BEING A
WOMAN

... Who's Had Enough!

Lynn B. Mann

The right of Lynn B. Mann to be identified as author
of this work has been asserted by her in accordance
with the Copyright, Designs and Patents Act 1988.

A CIP catalogue record for this book is available
from the British Library.

ISBN: 978-1-8381628-4-9

For Annie

CONTENTS

Author's Note

Being a Woman is a personal exploration and reflection on my experience of being a woman, and the cultural issues relating to that.

My decision to focus exclusively on the experience of being a woman is not a statement of disregard for other genders or identities. Rather, this book is written from the point of view of the lens through which I have navigated the world.

I acknowledge and respect the diverse range of identities and experiences that exist beyond the scope of these pages.

DEFINITIONS

To avoid any uncertainty, I've listed below my definitions of some of the terms I use throughout the book.

Patriarchal society: A culture that is organised in such a way that men hold more power and authority than women and there is a cultural bias towards, or privileging of, men. Also, a culture in which traditionally 'masculine' qualities (such as aggression, competitiveness and physical strength) are seen as desirable and superior.

Sexism: 'Prejudice, stereotyping, or discrimination, typically against women, on the basis of sex' (Oxford Dictionary).

Misogyny: I always thought this meant an open hatred of women, so it was relatively rare. However, although it can be this, it doesn't need to be as extreme for it to be misogyny: 'Dislike of, contempt for or ingrained prejudice against women' (Oxford Dictionary) or 'Feelings of hating women, or the belief that men are much better than women' (Cambridge Dictionary).

Chauvinist: 'Believing that, or behaving as if, women are naturally less important, intelligent, or able than men' (Cambridge Dictionary).

Sex: When I mention sex, I'm referring to biological sex.

Gender: When I mention gender, I'm referring to the expression of our sex through socially constructed roles and characteristics – 'gender norms'.

INTRODUCTION

I was in my mid-thirties. My son was a toddler, running around the kitchen, while I sat at the table eating lunch with my husband and my parents, who were visiting us for a few days. I felt tense and a bit apprehensive, but also excited. I was choosing my moment to tell them my news. My husband already knew.

At the time I was a full-time mum. After a variety of career paths in my twenties, including working as a researcher then a director in television, I trained as a fitness instructor, then stopped teaching classes when our son was born. In my mid-twenties I'd been keen to train as a psychotherapist, when I was offered a place on a sought-after university counselling studies degree course. I was also given the opportunity of a longer-term job as a researcher in television, which I had already been doing part-time.

I listened to all the voices of family and friends telling me to 'take the TV job'. It must have seemed so much more glamorous, a much better opportunity, and more of a certainty career-wise. At the time, there were very few counsellors in full-time employment, and it wasn't so commonplace for people to have counselling. Loudest of the voices telling me it was a 'no-brainer' was my dad, who implied that counselling was a bit 'airy-fairy' anyway.

I went with my conditioning, I went with the external pressure to do what *seemed* like the best option, the most sensible option. I didn't listen to the small voice inside me that was urging me to do what I knew I *really* wanted to do.

So, there I was, several major life events and many years on from that fork in the road, about to tell my parents that I was finally going to go to university to get a degree and become a therapist. I was also going to tell them I'd realised that this was what I should have chosen all those years before. That it felt like what I was meant to do. That it felt meaningful and purposeful for me.

However, I didn't get to the second part because the first bit went something like this.

Me: 'I've got something to tell you both.'

Expectant looks.

'I'm going back to education. I'm going to do the degree in counselling studies that I was going to do years ago. I'm going to train to become a psychotherapist.'

Mum nods, but doesn't say anything.

Dad says, 'What kind of money will you make at that, then?'

Me: 'Well, it depends where I end up working, but if I'm full-time, maybe around £25k a year.'

Dad scoffs, while continuing to eat his lunch, then says, laughing, 'Ha, you could make more than that as a lap dancer.'

I don't know what I said after that. I don't think I said very much. I think the conversation changed course, after I limply said something about this being what I really wanted to do, and I was looking forward to it, then I continued to eat my lunch.

However, I remember exactly how I felt. I felt humiliated. I felt shamed. I felt like I wanted to burst into tears. I think I felt like a little girl. And as I write this now and remember that scene, I feel the physical sensations again: my face flushed and I felt sick. I can still feel the physical tension throughout my body that it took for me to stay sitting in my chair that day when what I really wanted to do was burst into tears and run out of the kitchen.

.oOo.

The incident I've just detailed is seared on my memory, and I realise that it must paint my dad as a sexist boor, which he wasn't. He was a good man, and a good dad. I loved my dad very much, and I know he loved me: he wanted only the best for me, and for me to be happy.

So why, when my dad jokingly suggested that a better financial alternative to training as psychotherapist would be to become a lap dancer, didn't I say, 'What the hell are you talking about?' Or 'That's really hurtful.' Why didn't I speak up for myself? I was an adult. I liked to think of myself as a strong, capable woman who could handle herself. If someone was rude to me, I didn't just take it. But on this occasion, though, I said nothing. I'd been told that I'd be better off using my body to earn my living, letting men leer at me wearing virtually no clothes, rather than using my mind, and my natural empathy and compassion. I'd been cut to the core. I'd been humiliated and made to feel small, in my own home by a member of my own family ... and I said nothing.

Neither my mum nor my husband said anything to my dad either. (Of course, I understand why they didn't: they didn't want to 'spoil the atmosphere'; 'it was only a joke'; and of course, Dad was the authority figure.) For him to say something so outrageous and for it to be ignored by all of us seems unbelievable to me now. And why did my dad – an intelligent man, brought up to be respectful and decent, a family man who loved both his children and was really proud of me – think it was okay to say that to his daughter, even as a 'joke'?

You might think that this wasn't a big deal, or that I shouldn't have taken it so seriously, but that's because we have been taught to react this way, as women. That's how we've been conditioned: into seeing these kind of incidents as 'banter', not harmful or threatening, in any way. We've been conditioned to think of them as not demeaning, derogatory or personal – even if they *feel* that way to us.

Crucially, that's why it seemed like a big deal to me – because of how it made me feel. If I hadn't been so affected by it, if it hadn't really bothered me, if it hadn't really hurt me, then I wouldn't still remember it so vividly, and still get so churned up by it, over *twenty* years later.

As women, we've been programmed to discount our own experiences of sexism, of how things affect us individually, regardless of whether or not they would have the same effect on someone else in the same circumstances or situation. We don't speak up in case we're told we're 'too sensitive' or we 'can't take a joke' or we're 'being a bitch'. And some women don't speak up out of fear of being met with anger or violence. It doesn't matter whether other people think something is worth getting angry or upset about; only we know how these things affect us.

Many incidents throughout my life, like the one with my dad, have bothered me for a very long time. Often, this is because of my – and others' – lack of reaction to them. This is just one of a catalogue of incidents where I've felt an uncomfortable emotional or psychological response to the way I – or another woman – was treated, just because we are female.

For most of my life, I've had lots of unanswered – or even unasked – questions around this kind of stuff. Women in our society just put up with an awful lot of things that are supposed to be part of being a woman.

This book is about the multitude of things that we women tolerate, ignore, pretend we don't notice, or stay silent about – often at a cost to ourselves. From small, annoying things to huge, life-changing events, each woman will have experienced a similar series of events in their own life. I'm talking about times when you've felt vulnerable, humiliated, afraid, threatened, degraded, cheapened, ignored, sidelined, belittled or *lesser* – just for being female.

The book is also about the pressure we face daily to conform to prescribed roles and identities that we've been brainwashed into believing are 'the norm' and that we ought to aspire to: we risk disturbing the status quo and/or losing our sense of belonging if we don't play the game by the rules we've been given. From the way we dress, our hair, our faces, our bodies to the way we carry out our roles at work and the household burdens we carry, it's all up for scrutiny: we're judged and criticised online, in the media, in our homes and at work, and we're insidiously programmed to judge and criticise ourselves – and often other women – in the same way.

If you grew up in the Western world, you grew up in a sexist, patriarchal culture. It was all around us but we were largely blind to it. Nobody talked about it. We were left to swallow our discomfort, hurt, distaste or confusion at what we encountered, rather than society changing to align with what we deserve to experience as equal, valuable human beings.

For instance, many women of my generation grew up feeling that it wasn't right that between 1970 and 2015, when you turned the first page of the most popular newspapers in the country, you were confronted by a photo of a topless woman. Did we say anything about our discomfort, embarrassment or distaste? Maybe you did. I didn't. What I find hard to understand is, did none of our fathers, or older brothers – or, for God's sake, our mothers – think it was inappropriate for their daughters, or sisters, to have these images inflicted on them every day? Did it never occur to them that we might find them demeaning, humiliating or embarrassing, or that these images might give us the impression that this was the worth of a woman in the eyes of the world – a pair of breasts to look at? And what about our mothers? Didn't those images bother them?

Another occasion springs to mind. In my twenties, a man I'd only gone out with a few times pinned me by my throat to the wall of my flat in a fit of rage because I'd made a mildly sarcastic remark to him. So why did I spend the rest of the evening consoling him and telling him not to worry, saying that of course I'd still go out with him? (And I did, a couple of times more, before seeing the light.) Yet around this time, on the way to my part-time evening job in a bistro, I saw a guy pushing a woman around in the street, angry at her, and I shouted at him to leave her alone. I stood up for her but accepted worse treatment for myself – from someone I was in a relationship with. Confusing contradictions seemed to abound.

You're likely to have your own memories of times when you were angry, embarrassed or vulnerable, or even terrified. Times when you put up with poor treatment that you would have told a friend not to put up with. Why do we do it? And what does the accumulation of this type of thing over years and years do to your sense of yourself? How does it affect your sense of your own worth? How does it affect how you feel about, and treat, your body? Does it erode your ability to develop your own voice and express yourself fully? What does it do to your sense of your own power in the world, and your ability to create the life you want to live and become the person you want to be? How does it affect your self-confidence and self-esteem?

These types of incidents and experiences can have a big impact in all of these areas. However, we don't tend to connect our struggles with self-worth, self-esteem or confidence with sexism. We don't see all the subliminal messages and conditioning we've grown up with in our patriarchal society as related to these issues – but in fact, they are related. The two things are entangled.

An illustration of how these messages and conditioning affect our sense of our selves can be seen in the current endemic of eating disorders among girls and young women. Although much more is now known about eating disorders than thirty or forty years ago, their rates continue to rise and rise. More and more girls and young women have the same distorted relationship with food and their own bodies that women have struggled with for decades. Why haven't things changed for them? Why haven't we been able to change things for them through our experiences of the same problems, and the lessons we've learned in dealing with them?

Tragically, self-harm sits alongside eating disorders as one of the ways in which many teenage girls and young women now try to deal with the emotional and psychological turmoil of living in this world as a female. Why do these young souls, who have barely had time to learn about life and what it's all about, feel the need to harm themselves? Are we doing something wrong as a society? Is there anything we can do as individuals – in our families, in our schools and social circles – that could make a difference? And how are all of these self-destructive behaviours related to our conditioning as girls and women, brought up in a patriarchal society surrounded by sexism and inequality?

Our patriarchal conditioning is the anaesthetic that we, and generations of women before us, were drip-fed throughout our lives: it largely numbed us to the toxic sexism that we breathed in daily. It also enabled us to sleepwalk into prescribed gender roles and identities, whether or not they felt right for us. This conditioning allowed organisations and institutions to treat women as second-class citizens for a long time (and many still do) and meant that most women just accepted it. It also blinded us to the injustice in our homes, where women have always done (and most still do) the lion's share of housework, as well as childcare, even if both partners have a job outside the home. 'That's just the way it is', we were told.

But women have been growing more conscious of these things in recent years. Sometimes shocking cases in the media regarding individuals or organisations generate collective outrage, and another crack appears in the wall of patriarchy. The tremors of movements such as #MeToo reverberate throughout today's society – unfortunately, this comes hand in hand with men saying 'NAMALT (not all men are like this)' (maybe not, but a lot are!) or 'it's not that bad' (it is). Still women have to contend daily with sexist behaviours and attitudes all around us. Still rates of assault and violence against women and girls climb, while conviction rates fall, and we still find ourselves on the hamster wheel of patriarchy, running to keep up – or running for our lives.

Some of these things have bothered me for decades, and some are more recent concerns, especially since I had my daughter. And now I've reached the point where I can no longer tolerate them festering away inside me. This book is my best attempt at trying to make sense of the world we live in, by exploring these issues, trying to understand more about them, and see them with fresh eyes. I've never vocalised my thoughts and feelings around these things, or tried to answer some of these questions for myself, until now. To be honest, I probably never would have if it hadn't been for an article I read one Sunday morning last year, while I was sitting in bed having a cup of tea.

At that point, I'd already published two books and had started working on a third, which was nothing to do with what I'm writing about here. That Sunday morning, a shocking headline caught my eye, and I read the whole article. It was called 'Nudes, porn, abuse – the toxic culture in UK classrooms'[1] (I'll talk about it in more detail in Chapter 6). As the mother of a daughter of thirteen, I was horrified. It triggered a need in me to do some research. I almost couldn't let myself believe that the article was true. I thought, 'That can't be right'. Surely girls and boys in their teens are more equal now. They must be aware of the concepts of self-respect, respecting

---

1   Lucy Bannerman (15 April 2021),
    https://www.thetimes.co.uk/article/nudes-porn-abuse-the-toxic-culture-in-uk-classrooms-fl3m7wjmg

others, dignity, etc., regardless of their sex or gender. Surely?

But it seemed I was wrong. When I did more research, I found that article after article, study after study, book after book, gave me a clearer picture on where girls and women really are in terms of equality. What I found, instead of allaying my fears, intensified them. This opened a floodgate of questions. I felt that I needed to try to understand why things hadn't changed in the way I thought they had. I also felt that I needed to figure out what, if anything, I could do to make a difference.

That was the catalyst for me to write this book. The dam has burst, and I'm sweeping you up and taking you with me on the journey so we can try to find some of the answers together and, crucially, see how we can help to create different experiences of being a woman – for ourselves, and for the girls and women who will follow us. (Actually, for future generations of boys and men too, because, as I'll discuss later, this isn't all their fault.)

What we experience today, as boys and girls and men and women living in Western society, is the accumulation of centuries of ingrained attitudes, structures and systems. If our culture is toxic for girls and women, then it's toxic for boys and men too. Boys and men also need different experiences than they're having currently. We all deserve better. We all need to be part of the solution. We need to do it differently... but how?

Let's look at where we are currently, how we got here, and how we might be able to create different experiences going forward, to make living in this culture feel less frustrating and hopeless.

This book is intended to make you look at things with fresh eyes, from a new perspective. I want you to think about your own life and your own experiences. Once you start to see some of the things I have begun to see, you can't unsee them.

I'm not approaching this politically or academically. I'm not an expert. My only qualifications to write this book are having lived over fifty years on this planet, experiencing life as a girl, then a woman, in a sexist, patriarchal culture.

I'm here to connect with you – woman to woman – to see if you might also have had enough:

- enough of trying to contort yourself into the one-size-fits-all roles and rules ascribed to us from birth by a society designed by and for men;
- enough of being constantly judged – and trained to judge ourselves even more harshly;
- enough of being objectified as a collection of body parts, and having our worth equated with how we look;
- enough of expending time and energy in staying on the treadmill that promises us we must meet society's standards of an ideal woman/wife/mother;
- enough of the unfair expectations on women around household burdens and caring roles; and
- enough of the cultural attitudes that tolerate and diminish everyday sexist behaviours, and their impacts.

In a nutshell, I've had enough of the ways in which women are treated unfairly, inhumanely or as *less than* the magnificent human beings we are.

Maybe you have too.

What can we do about it? Let's find out.

CHAPTER 1

Where I'm coming from

Let me backtrack and give you an overview of where I'm coming from historically, before I start to explore our collective experience of being a woman.

I started this book with what I think is quite a glaring example of sexism in my own family. My dad, however, would not have realised how sexist it was of him to say this, or how hurtful or humiliating it felt for me; he too was moulded and conditioned by a sexist culture in a patriarchal society. It seemed that he was completely blind to this, though – and practically all his generation seem to be, both men and women.

My parents grew up in poverty in Glasgow, Scotland, in the 1940s and 1950s, both in families of five children. Each of them lost a parent in childhood.

My dad spent a lot of his early years with his two much older brothers. They were all brought up in a violent, sexist, alcohol-soaked culture. His mother worked long hours as a cleaner to provide for them all. My dad was fiercely proud of, loyal to, protective of and loving towards his mother, who lived into her eighties. He always appreciated what she had done for him, and he looked after her financially for the rest of her life as soon as he was able to.

My maternal grandmother died of tuberculosis when my mum was eleven, after my mum had nursed her for two years. That meant that my mum missed a lot of school. She then became the 'mother' of the house and missed even more school due to looking after her siblings. She barely had any parental input or presence, as her father had to work long hours to keep the family together.

My mum and dad accepted and internalised all the messages they received about women and men and their roles and how they were supposed to behave. These were completely ingrained in both of them. As far as I could see, they then perpetuated these – more or less unquestioningly – throughout their lives, unwittingly conditioning me in the same way.

I spent the first eighteen months of my life living with my parents in my paternal grandmother's council house in what could be described as a rough area of Glasgow. Then my dad, an electrician at the time, started the first of many entrepreneurial ventures, and managed to get a mortgage to buy the first house that had ever been owned in either of their families. We moved to a brand-new two-bedroomed semi-detached house in a cul-de-sac on a new estate out of the city. Things were looking up!

Over the next sixteen years there followed three house moves, each one to a larger house than the last, as my dad bought petrol stations, car showrooms, a car wash, a pub and finally a hotel on the West coast of Scotland, where he and my mum retired to.

Through his ambition, vision, sheer determination, and hard work, my dad ended up pulling us all into a very different world than the one he grew up in. By sheer will, he created a different life for his family. I say 'he', but of course he was completely facilitated and supported by my mum. He wouldn't have been able to achieve all he did without her unwavering love and care – and the fact that she shouldered 100% of the running of the household, housework and childcare, as well as owning a baby clothes shop for five years while I was in my teens, then running the hotel. However, he was the major decision-maker and the driving force: so much so that he bought our new houses – every single one of them, and the hotel – *then* came home to tell my mum what he had done.

I am outlining all this to say that I was fortunate to have a far more privileged childhood than either of them could have imagined when they were children. They made a point of saying they didn't want to spoil my brother (born when I was eight) and me, but they probably did. However, I was still programmed by societal messaging, through them, about how a girl should look and behave, how I should dress, and what was 'ladylike'. I grew up with the same expectations around gender expression and roles that they had. My parents never doubted, questioned or let go of these.

The patriarch

We never questioned the fact that my dad was the boss in our house, the traditional 'head of the family'. I assumed this was the case in everyone's houses. Why wouldn't I? Growing up in the UK in the 1970s and 1980s, the families represented in most TV programmes were just like ours: a mum, a dad and kids, where Dad was the boss and Mum was a housewife.

All our neighbours had the same set-up, and the children I knew at school did too. I must have known somebody who came from a family where the parents were separated or divorced, but I honestly can't remember any at all, not until I was well into my twenties. When I look back now, my early years look like living in the 1950s. That's what Mum and Dad had been programmed to create.

Mum had Dad's dinner ready for him when he came in the door from work. I knew when Dad was about to arrive home because there would be a flurry of activity: Mum would simultaneously tidy up, finish making dinner, fix her hair and reapply her lipstick, while telling me to do something to help, keep quiet, or get out the way!

There was a palpable tension in the air. Not because my dad was violent or aggressive towards my mum; he never was. He was the opposite: very loving and affectionate towards her. According to my mum, 'he had been working hard all day' so he deserved to have a fuss made of him when he got home. Even although she'd also been working hard all day, cleaning, cooking, food shopping and caring for their children.

She didn't question what was expected of her as a woman, a wife and a mother. She was playing the role of the model wife from the 1950s, and he was playing his role of the breadwinner – the roles they'd both been brought up to aspire to.

I don't remember thinking there was anything wrong with this scenario, or questioning it, but it must have registered with me on some level that something about it wasn't right because I remember it so vividly, and I noticed it at the time and was bothered by it.

The swinging 60s seemed to bypass my parents entirely. I'm not sure if they were too conservative, or too scared, to be part of it, or if they were just focused on bettering their lives, on following their programming.

More or less, though, they lived their lives as they had been moulded and conditioned to. Then, because they unquestioningly perpetuated these rules, I was steeped in the same attitudes and saw the same behaviours play out as I was growing up. In my dad's lifetime he was never challenged as the patriarch of the family.

My parents and I were victims of the same ingrained societal conditioning around sex and gender roles. It was only when I was in my late teens that I started to be more aware of this and began to notice not only some of the inequalities of sex and gender roles, but also the privileged existence we'd led as a middle-class nuclear family living in a decent area in Scotland.

CHAPTER 2

Looking like a woman: body image

I would say that our collective fixation on body image is currently the biggest affliction of most women living in the Western world. Obviously, this is inextricably linked to our patriarchal conditioning and sexism. Women's issues with the way our bodies look are pervasive, and – for many of us – consume a disproportionate amount of our time, attention and energy. Whether they're unhappy with their size, shape, weight, stomach, thighs, breasts, arms, skin, face, hair, teeth or nails, most women have some degree of dislike, or even hatred, for one or many things about the way they look.

Of course, some men do too, but it's much more widespread and ingrained in women, and that's my focus in this book. Women and girls are given the message over and over again by society, since virtually the day we're born, that how we look is what matters most about us.

Marketing to, selling to, and perpetuating women's dissatisfactions, insecurities and fears around the way they look, and how they measure up to societal ideals, has evolved into a colossal money-making machine. The beauty, fashion, skincare, cosmetics, exercise, diet, pharmaceutical and surgical industries all thrive on women not liking the way they look and wanting to look different: wanting to look the way we've been *told* we should look by these very industries. This model is designed to show women that they can look younger, prettier, sexier – *better*. That who you are as a woman, your value to society, or even your inherent value, is dependent on this, whatever the cost to you – financially, emotionally, psychologically, to your sense of self, or to your dignity and your soul.

Most of us have, or still do, buy into some or all of it. Very few of us are immune to it. Many women don't choose the ultimate way to become the ideal – plastic surgery – because they can't afford it, but many who don't, would if they could.

But what are we buying into? Is it youth? Is it perfection? Is it being a better version of ourselves? We all have our own motivations for chasing the illusions we're sold. However, we can take the first step away from this madness by waking up to what we're doing, by understanding the structures and systems we live in, so we can see them for what they are. We need to be aware of the ways we've blindly followed our societal programming if we want to do things differently.

Societal programming

We grow up surrounded by images – online, in women's magazines, on tv, in movies, in advertisements – of perfectly preened, beautifully dressed, artistically made-up, slim, attractive women. Our subconscious interprets these into three rules for us to adhere to in relation to our own body image:

1. That's the way a woman is *supposed* to look.

2. You should aspire to look like that, so that's your goal as a woman.

3. You must constantly assess how far short you are from – or near you are to – achieving that goal. You must also assess other women to see where you think they are on the scale, and in comparison to you.

As a child, and as a young woman, as you went about your life, messages about your body and body image were being programmed into you, every day, in every area of your life. You are not to blame for this, because you played no part in it. You were born into this set-up, just like everyone around you. How could you see? How could you know?

It doesn't really matter that, as you grow up and talk to friends about body image, or see and hear discussions or read new information about these issues, and begin to realise that your worth isn't defined by your size, shape, weight or looks. *All of that is conscious thought. Your subconscious is still programmed with all the images and ideals of who you were supposed to become that you absorbed over years as you were growing up.*

This creates in you something called cognitive dissonance. I'm going to talk about this several times throughout this book, and will go into it in more detail in Chapter 11, because it's very important, as it's the key to unlocking the mental cage of societal conditioning.

It's not so much what we're *told* when we're younger, or we begin to see as we get older, that shapes us and our thoughts and behaviours. It's what we see and hear daily, over years, as we grow up. All the subliminal messaging is what brainwashes us. For us to really see things differently, and change our attitudes and perspectives, and change how we feel about ourselves and to alter our behaviour, we have to *see the programming for what it is – and consciously change it*. Otherwise, the new messages get discounted or fight against the old, ingrained ones in your psyche. Our subconscious programming keeps on going, wreaking havoc in our lives – for years, for decades, or for our whole lives.

The start of changing it is just being aware of it: to realise that you've been soaked in it and that it's formed your attitude towards yourself, to women and men in general, and to life and the way you live it. Most of us are unaware that we're looking at and judging ourselves – and other women – *through the lens of our societal conditioning.* Because of this, many of our thoughts aren't our own. We think they are, and they feel like they are, but actually we've taken on the thoughts of our programming as our own.

When you see this and become aware of it, you can break its spell over you. We'll look at what comes next in Chapter 11 later. For now, it's enough that you can see it, and you begin to notice your own attitudes to yourself and your body. Be alert to your internal dialogue: consider how much of it has been programmed into you.

In relation to your own body image, try to catch your thoughts about the way you look, or thoughts that trigger particular behaviours: for instance, feeling the need to change yourself physically, maybe through controlling your weight, or through exercise, or through ruminating on physical aspects of yourself you don't like. Notice the thoughts that accompany these. What are you telling yourself about who you are and how you feel about your body? Ask yourself why you want to look different – is this to meet some standard of your own? Where has that standard come from? What do you want to achieve by meeting it? How will it make you feel about yourself? Who will benefit from the change? Are you doing it so you feel more 'worthy', more 'perfect' or more desirable, or to feel that you fit in, that you belong?

The list of reasons for us to hate aspects of our own bodies is endless, but the bottom line is: it's about feeling that you're not enough the way you are. That somehow, you're not okay. That you're not reaching or maintaining the goals that you believed you were meant to achieve. You're judging yourself harshly, and you want to do something to make yourself different.

The roots of judging ourselves

When you were young, perhaps you couldn't imagine growing up to look like one of the slim, attractive, vivacious, popular girls or women that you saw on TV or elsewhere in the media. Perhaps your self-esteem wasn't great, and perhaps this caused problems for you in relationships or socially, *because* you measured yourself against an ideal that you thought you could never attain.

On the other hand, perhaps as a child you *could* see yourself growing into one of those women you saw in the media. Then your self-esteem might have been reasonably good, as you'd feel that you could achieve the goal of becoming like these women. You could see yourself as one. Perhaps the pressure of achieving that goal, along with the other pressures of life, caused problems for you in some other way, though. Maybe it's contributed to a battle with your weight, or an eating disorder, or poor mental health. You might have spent your life permanently on a diet, or you might have always been very conscious of what you eat so you could stay slim. (I don't know many women who *don't* have some level of conscious, tense, unhealthy, chaotic, disciplined or disordered relationship to food. And I can't think of any men I know who do. Although that doesn't mean that there aren't any. It's just much more endemic in women.)

The bottom line though, is that whether or not you could see yourself in those 'ideal' women, you were messed up either way. What does that tell you about the relationship between societal ideals around body image and being a woman? Women often define themselves by their attitude to their body and food. I could write a whole book about this, but to illustrate this, my own attitude to my body and food has been shaped in the following way.

As a child, since I had a really short haircut and was very tall for my age, I looked like a boy (people in shops often mistook me for one). I changed schools twice between the age of seven and twelve, and never really felt that I fitted in. I was bullied badly by a boy when I was eight or nine, then when I was the last girl to be picked for dancing practice at school, the last boy left refused to pick me because I 'was like a boy'.

When I was a teenager, just before all the clothes shops started their 'tall' ranges, I couldn't find jeans that were long enough for me, or shoes that fitted properly; I had to stuff my feet into shoes that were a size too small for most of my teens and twenties. So, as you can imagine, my body image wasn't the best.

There was absolutely nobody I saw – in my life, or in the media or films – that I saw myself in. I felt that perhaps if I could make myself look different, I might be able to fit in more, be more 'normal' looking.

I started my first diet aged about fourteen. Inevitably, lots of days, I'd end up caving in to cravings and buying crisps and sweets. And although I was a normal size during my school years, not overweight, I always felt fat. I always felt too big, and too clumsy, because I was taller than everyone else.

It was no surprise, then, that by the time I was in my late teens, I loathed my body, and had begun what was to be a ten-year battle with bulimia. I cycled between rigid and chaotic eating patterns, and my weight seesawed between normal/slim and two or three stones overweight, sometimes within the space of a couple of months.

I finally managed to deal with my attitude to food when I got pregnant with my first child, although I still ended up yo-yo dieting for years afterwards. I'm relieved to say that a couple of decades later, I have a much healthier relationship with food than I've ever had. I rarely even weigh myself now, as I'm no longer obsessed with what I weigh, or my size. My life, and my sense of self-worth, don't revolve around these things.

My body image still has ups and downs. Like most of us, I'm still prone to focusing on my negatives rather than my positives. I do feel, though, that I'm developing a different perspective to my appearance now: that I'm coming to accept and appreciate my body as it is. I'm learning to focus more on health and well-being and looking after and being grateful for my body, and how lucky I am to be relatively fit and healthy, rather than on the things I'd like to change. However, I still have to consciously redirect my thinking away from automatically judging myself harshly.

The role sexism plays in women's body image

If boys in a patriarchal, sexist society grow up seeing women's bodies viewed as objects to be lusted over or assessed, understandably, most will accept this and think that this is 'just the way things are'. They have been societally programmed to think this way. They will also have seen the women around them accepting this, or even perpetuating it, by striving to fit into their role and be the 'ideal' woman.

So, if girls and women grow up seeing this, and feeling the judging gaze of boys, then men, we internalise this and learn to judge ourselves, and each other, by the same standards. We learn to see ourselves and other women through the eyes of men, through *their* assessment of our attractiveness. We objectify ourselves – and other women – in the same way that we see men judging women. It's all down to our brainwashing, which we're unaware of, because it has played out all around us since the day we were born. And we can't see it for what it is until we understand what's been happening.

Obviously, because we're mere mortals, we can't achieve society's idea of the ideal woman, but many women spend days, months and years trying to, then beating ourselves up when we fall short. Sadly, the only solace we get lies in judging ourselves against other women and finding them wanting in some area. This makes us think that we're 'winning' the game, beating them. This can make us feel less bad about our own perceived shortcomings – at least, temporarily.

We do this largely unconsciously, and we don't mean any harm to other women by it, as it's not about them, it's about us. It's about our own fragile ego trying to make ourselves feel better about our perceived flaws and failings, to reassure ourselves that we're as attractive, or fashionable, or sexy, or *whatever,* as we hope we are, or as we want to be. It's about our fears and inadequacies.

And we do this automatically unless we become aware of it. Awareness is the first step in seeing the game for what it is, in seeing the web of demands and rules that have been spun around us. Next, we can begin to recognise the part we play in perpetuating it. The end goal is for us to develop a healthy sense of our own body, and to start to appreciate all that our body does for us, and to raise our self-esteem so that it's based on who we are, not just the way we look. I'll go into this in more detail in Chapter 12.

Disordered eating from disordered body image

Developing an eating disorder is a way of attacking, of turning on, your own body: attacking it and/or trying to control it, either by starving it or by abusing it with excess food or excess weight. Nourishing ourselves with healthy food, which is one of the most caring things we can do for ourselves, becomes a minefield, a war zone, and something that can set up a struggle within us that can last most of our lives. How sad is that?

I think this will be a familiar story for many of you. Unfortunately, girls and young women are being set up to hate their own bodies and to constantly strive for an ideal that they can never meet. They've seen us doing it yet they still look at themselves through the lens of a sexist society – and social media has only made this worse. How are we going to help our daughters avoid years of self-loathing or, at the very least, constant anxiety and tension around how they look?

An American university study into disordered eating[2] revealed the following stats, and the UK follows a similar pattern:

- 57% of women had tried to lose weight in the past year: two-thirds said they diet 'all or most of the time'.[3]
- 75% of American women report disordered eating behaviours or symptoms consistent with eating disorders.
- 67% are trying to lose weight.
- 53% of women on a diet are already at a healthy weight.
- 39% of women say that concerns about what they eat or weigh impact their happiness.

In the UK, a 2022 NHS report stated that 'The NHS continues to see record-high numbers of young people for eating disorders.'[4]

We all need to eat to live, yet food can become emotionally loaded for many girls and women. A healthy

---

2   University of North Carolina at Chapel Hill. 'Three out of four American women have disordered eating, survey suggests.' ScienceDaily. www.sciencedaily.com/releases/2008/04/080422202514.htm

3   Rachel Moss (March 2016), 'Two-thirds of Brits are on a diet "most of the time"'. The Huffington Post UK. https://www.huffingtonpost.co.uk/2016/03/10/majority-brits-are-on-a-diet-most-of-the-time_n_9426086.html

4   NHS England (7 March 2022) 'NHS treating record number of young people for eating disorders'. www.england.nhs.uk/2022/03/nhs-treating-record-number-of-young-people-for-eating-disorders/

appetite is encouraged in boys and men, but not necessarily in girls and women. Also, girls grow up with female family and friends on diets and talking about the things they don't like about their bodies, and their weight, or how they look.

Because of my struggles when I was younger, I've been very careful over the years not to talk about weight or diets in front of my daughter. I didn't want to give her the impression that women are just about what we weigh or how we look. However, I don't know if it'll have made any difference. My daughter has grown up with and has absorbed attitudes, information and influences about weight since she was born: at school, with friends, on TV and on social media: she has been bombarded by messages encouraging her to equate her worth with how she looks, and in particular with how slim she is.

This societal conditioning is still going on for younger generations. Thankfully, there seems to be a growing number of girls and women promoting body positivity, but sadly they have to compete with all the channels promoting the old messages.

Self-harm as annihilation

It seems to me that self-harm is the epitome of a physical expression of self-loathing – that girls and young women might use it as a physical outlet for emotional and mental chaos. It's an external, physical response to, or outlet for, emotional or psychological pain, an attempt to gain a sense of control, or a release of stress. For some, this pain may be caused by feeling that they have fallen short of all that they think they're supposed to conform to, or by feeling that they are oppressed by societal conditioning. It may be a type of rebellion against societal messaging, standards and rules, that young people are aware of and instinctively feel are wrong.

A recent article in medical journal *The Lancet* found 'the increased prevalence [of self-harm] was most notable in women and girls aged 16–24 years, in whom prevalence had increased from 6.5% to 19.7% in only 4 years.'[5] Could there be a correlation between this and the burgeoning influence of social media in young people's lives?

The battle within

Many girls and young women feel bad about themselves or are confused. They have feelings that they don't know what to do with, so they stuff them down, or throw them up, or starve themselves, or self-harm to avoid these feelings, to escape them, or as a physical outlet for their internal pain.

The vast majority of the young people who turn to these coping mechanisms are female, and this is no coincidence. Of course, our body image and our

---

5   Sally McManus et al. (June 2019) 'Prevalence of non-suicidal self-harm and service contact in England, 2000–14: repeated cross-sectional surveys of the general population.' Lancet 6(7): 573–81.
www.thelancet.com/journals/lanpsy/article/PIIS2215-0366(19)30188-9/fulltext

indoctrination into the patriarchal system set up to endorse, perpetuate and police women is going to be our battleground as we grow and mature. However, some girls and women turn inwards and make the battle an internal one, against ourselves, which is more societally acceptable and convenient than turning outwards to battle the structures and systems that want women to stick to the rules.

Often, turning the battle inwards is the easier option for us. It maintains the status quo. It means we don't have to challenge individuals, systems, organisations or social norms. We get to retain the illusion that we're reasonably okay, even if we're not, because we're playing by the rules, and that lets us stay in the game. We just need to strive to fix *ourselves* rather than anything external. We have to convince ourselves that the wrongness we know exists is within us, rather than around us, sewn into the fabric of the world we live in. We still get to belong – as long as we don't try to unpick any threads.

War paint

Another aspect of body image is cosmetics. Why do most women feel the need to wear make-up? I've worn it every day since I was a teen, apart from maybe the odd day when I was ill. I wore more make-up in my twenties than I do now (today I use mascara, lipstick and foundation), and I've stuck to more or less the same colours, tones and brands for decades.

But why do I still feel that I *need* to put make-up on every day? And it does feel like a need. Even though I tell my teenage daughter that she doesn't need make-up, that she looks lovely without it, and she can choose whether or not to wear it, I don't lead by example. I just wouldn't go out without wearing mascara and lipstick – although I reckon I could manage without foundation.

To me, wearing make-up is not about trying to appear attractive to the opposite sex – but it probably was when I started wearing it. Now, I wear make-up because I prefer the way I look with it than without it. Like choosing a favourite outfit to wear because I feel good in it, or it's really comfortable. I also feel more confident when I'm wearing make-up. It acts as my persona, my mask.

I don't think I'd choose to wear make-up if applying it took a lot of time, but it only takes me a few minutes. But how much am I kidding myself on about my motivations for wearing it? Am I still doing what I think I need to do to be accepted, to look feminine, or more attractive, or to conform to ideals of enhancing myself? What do I think it adds to me or turns me into? Who would I be without it?

Some girls and women wear more make-up, and I always think that it must take them a lot of time to apply. For me, that would be fine for a special occasion, but if it's every day, I imagine it must feel like some kind of tyranny to feel that you 'have to' do it.

When it comes to make-up (like everything else!), it's up to you. Nobody should be bullied, shamed, or told what to do or not do by others, whether this is society, a partner, current trends or the media. Do what makes you feel good, fits in with your lifestyle, and allows you to feel like yourself. But perhaps it would be good for those of us who wear make-up to be honest with ourselves about why we wear it and what we think we get from it. (And to be aware that wearing make-up is yet another expectation of us as women).

The ageing woman

Western society has long been recognised as ageist, due to its undervaluing of older adults and the under-representation of positive older adult role models. We live in a youth-obsessed culture. The West is often unfavourably compared with Eastern cultures, which tend to view older people as valuable for their experience and wisdom.

However, even though in our culture men suffer from ageist attitudes, women are treated far worse, and there are many more negative stereotypes about older women. There's a double standard: men are often viewed as becoming more distinguished or attractive as they grow older (the silver fox), but women are more likely to become invisible or to be seen as less valuable as they age, presumably because we are seen as less attractive or less 'useful'.

Older women experience discrimination due to gendered ageism in various aspects of life, including in the workplace, media representation, and in healthcare settings. However, in a continuation of the societal pressures on us as younger women, the predominant way in which women are the victims of ageist attitudes relates to how we look as we age.

In Western media and the entertainment industries, there is a significant bias toward youth and beauty. A study in 2013 found that just 18% of UK television presenters over fifty are women.[6] An analysis of the most popular films and television shows from 2010 to 2020 by the organisation *See Jane* found that 'on-screen ageism persists and is particularly evident among on-screen women aged 50+. Just 1 in 4 characters who are 50+ are women.[7] This reinforces stereotypes about women's value being tied to their appearance.

Older women working in film, television, fashion, cosmetics and the beauty industry often face challenges securing opportunities compared to male counterparts. Unless, however, these opportunities are to promote anti-ageing products. That's an 'acceptable' thing for an older woman to do – to strive to look younger. To demonstrate that you don't need to look your age. To help us all avoid looking the age we really are for as long as possible. Isn't it seen as the ultimate compliment to say, on finding out

---

6   Jane Martinson, speaking to Miriam O'Reilly (May 2013), 'Just 18% of UK television presenters over 50 are women, study finds.' The Guardian, https://www.theguardian.com/media/2013/may/15/female-tv-presenters-ageism-sexism

7   'Women over 50: The right to be seen on screen: executive summary.' www.seejane.org, https://seejane.org/research-informs-empowers/women-over-50-report/

an older woman's age, 'Oh, but you don't look it'? Actress Jamie Lee Curtis recently spoke about how much she hates the term 'anti-ageing' because 'it represents a magic fix to the ageing process and portrays natural ageing as undesirable'.[8] She says that she is instead pro-ageing: where ageing is about our life experience, the lessons we've learned, getting to know and understand ourselves better, and getting to live the life we want to live – none of which is dependent on how we look.

Women in their fifties, sixties and beyond can expect to meet a new set of stereotypes and expectations. Let your hair go grey? You'll probably be told that you'd look younger if you dyed it. You're expected to 'dress your age', as if suddenly many clothes would be inappropriate, particularly any that might reveal a glimpse of ageing, wrinkled flesh. We're supposed to be ashamed of our ageing skin, our ageing faces and our ageing bodies – when the alternative to ageing is to be *dead*.

Nobody escapes ageing! It's a natural phenomenon, so we may as well accept it – or even embrace it. Let's stick two fingers up to these societal messages – we've earned the right to. With all the crap we've put up with over our lives, women have earned the right to age however the hell

---

8   S. Sethuraman (July 2023), 'I am pro-aging': Jamie Lee Curtis says she wants to get rid of the term 'anti-aging.'
https://scoop.upworthy.com/i-am-pro-aging-jamie-lee-curtis-says-she-wants-to-get-rid-of-the-term-anti-aging-566531-566531-566531

we want. Stuff ageing gracefully – how about ageing disgracefully?

Ageism directed at women turns what could be the most fulfilling and enjoyable time of our lives – when we have time to pursue our own agenda, do what we want to do and look after ourselves – into a time to be feared and dreaded, knowing that we are still expected to conform to society's expectations and age the ideal way a woman should age – that is, not at all.

It's up to us to reframe ageing for ourselves. To think about what we want our older years to look like, rather than worrying about how we'll look. To care more about just being comfortable in our own skin, than any accumulation of wrinkles on it. Let's lead by example and give ourselves a break. The young women and girls who follow us might be grateful that we're giving them 'permission' to do the same – and we get to have a more vibrant, fun life in the process.

CHAPTER 3

Society's straightjackets – designed in a snug fit for women

Body image is only one aspect of women's societal programming. We're also programmed around our gender identity, roles, relationships, and in our family expectations and responsibilities, and career options and aspirations.

In the past, women were often portrayed as one-dimensional characters in film or TV programmes, in stereotyped roles, usually as a love interest for the main male character, not as a character in their own right. Female characters were usually led by the males, and they followed their dictates. Any strong female characters were usually portrayed in a negative light often as being aggressive, bullying, hard, angry or emotionless – traditionally, dominant male characteristics. The Bechdel test was developed to 'analyse female presence in film by questioning (1) if there are at least two women; (2) if they have a conversation in the film; (3) and if the conversation relates to a topic other than men.'9 Many well-known films fail the test, including *A Star is Born*, *Elvis* and even Disney's *Mulan*.

I love it that about ten years ago, when American actress Reese Witherspoon was sick of reading script after script where her part was merely a support to the main male character, she set up her own production company so she could make films with strong female lead characters, as she could see that these were lacking in Hollywood. She has since produced several female-focused blockbusters, including *Gone Girl*, *Wild* and *Where the Crawdads Sing*. (Incidentally, her company was so successful that she recently sold it for $900 million.)

And when Geena Davis realised how few female characters there were in children's TV programmes and films, she set up the Geena Davis Institute on Gender in Media to raise awareness of this among TV executives and filmmakers. Her company advocates for women and 'works to mitigate unconscious bias while creating equality, fostering inclusion and reducing negative stereotyping in entertainment and media'.[10]

---

9   Abby Connolly (September 2023), 'Making films that pass the Bechdel test is essential to realistically and fairly representing women in the media.' Chip Chick, https://www.chipchick.com/2023/09/given-the-times-were-living-in-now-making-films-that-pass-the-bechdel-test-is-essential-to-realistically-and-fairly-representing-women-in-the-media.html

10 https://seejane.org/about-us/

Whether in film, on TV, in magazines, in adverts or online, we see fewer women than men represented to start with, but the women we see usually conform to the airbrushed, perfected idea of what a woman should look like, and how she should behave, and what her role in society ought to be – for her to be successful, admired, or even loved. These images are everywhere, in every area of our lives, and as we saw in Chapter 2, we're so used to them that we don't realise that they're burrowing into our psyche at every turn, affecting us psychologically, emotionally and spiritually.

The beauty industry, the fashion industry and the diet and exercise industries are the most obvious producers of the marketing that plays into our subconscious programming that we're not okay as we are, that we need a certain dress, handbag or eyeshadow to be one step closer to being the perfect woman. This can be seen in everything we're marketed to, in every area of our lives. The subliminal messages we're programmed with growing up ensure that these companies' huge marketing budgets hit the targets they're meant to. And for us, buying into whatever they're selling can make us feel that we've made some progress towards our ideals.

Being brainwashed into seeing our worth as only lying in how we look is only one aspect of our programming as girls and women. It also happens regarding marriage, motherhood and careers: we are told how we should carry out each of our roles *if we are to be seen as successful at them.*

Women learn from birth that society has certain expectations of us in order to belong. Belonging is a deep need in humans. We're hard-wired to seek it and hold on to it. We feel fear, anxiety and often shame if we feel that we're threatening our sense of belonging by not doing what we feel we're supposed to.

Recognising the messages

How many times have you been told 'Smile, love, it might never happen' as you go about your day, minding your own business and possibly using your grey matter to think about something important/interesting/ urgent?

Society tells us that we need to be alert and ready to respond with a smile, particularly to any man we encounter. Look happy, be nice (especially to men), don't be aggressive (especially to men), be ladylike (i.e. don't burp, fart or speak too loudly or, heaven forbid, dominate a conversation). Let men dominate conversations and keep smiling when they do. It's okay to show that you're smart, so long as you don't make a man look stupid in the process. If a man makes himself look stupid, help him save his injured ego in any way you can think of. Be good and kind and sweet, and gauge other people's (especially men's) opinions before you express any of your own.

Be sexy, but don't be slutty – except in the bedroom, where the sluttier you are, the better. (And the word 'slut' itself is used to judge a woman's value relative to her sexual experience, or her choice of clothes, or her responses to male attention.) Be attractive but don't be too full of yourself; being over-confident puts you in the firing line to be called 'hard', a 'bitch' or a 'ball-breaker'. The type of clothing you wear, and how much cleavage/leg/midriff/whatever, you show, should be appropriate to the circumstances, and if you're in a relationship, maybe you should only wear what your boyfriend/partner/husband is happy or comfortable with you wearing.

Some of these might seem extreme, but I'm sure you can recognise many of them from what you've seen growing up, or in the media. Most Hollywood movies from the 1950s until just a few years ago contained these sexist messages – and many still do.

So, even if you can't recognise much of this in your life now, think about how many of these messages might be lingering in your subconscious from your childhood, or in the minds of the people you see on a daily basis – male and female.

Sexist clichés and stereotypes

We've also grown up with sexist clichés and stereotypes woven into the fabric of our lives, often without recognising that they are sexist stereotypes. And they still surround us. They are harmful constructs that perpetuate gender inequality and limit women's potential as individuals. They oversimplify and generalise the roles, behaviours and attributes of women (and sometimes of men too).

Stereotypes of women seek to confine us to traditional roles. We're often portrayed or described as overly emotional, dependent or weak (physically, mentally and/or emotionally). Sexist stereotypes do men no favours either, as they are pressured from birth to conform to ideals of dominance, strength and lack of visible emotion ('keeping a stiff upper lip'). These clichés reinforce harmful power dynamics, and if we want to achieve true gender equality, we need to break free from them.

The continued use of these stereotypes is something that most women have seen or have had to deal with. We may not notice the following, or think of them as sexist tropes, but we see them represented around us every day:

- 'Overly emotional and irrational' suggests that women are less rational than men, and this undermines their capacity for logical thinking and decision-making.
- 'Working mothers': it's often unfairly implied that working mothers are less committed to their jobs than working fathers or other women; that they have divided loyalties or attention; or that they are in some way a liability for employers because they have to balance work and their family.
- 'Women are bad drivers': this implies that women are less skilled at driving than men, perpetuating the idea that one gender is innately better at certain activities.
- 'The man of the house' positions men as the ultimate authority figure in a household, marginalising women's decision-making and contributions.
- 'Locker-room talk': dismissing offensive and derogatory language about women as 'locker-room

talk' minimises the harm caused by engaging in and perpetuating objectifications of women, and disrespectful behaviour.

- 'Fragile femininity': this portrays women as more sensitive than men, more easily overwhelmed, or as needing constant protection and care because they are helpless.

These are just a few examples, but they show how ingrained sexist clichés and stereotypes are in our lives. The messages we soak up shape our behaviours, our attitudes, our opinions of others, and our thoughts about ourselves and our lives. Until we become aware this is happening, we do all this blindly, and ignore any feelings of discomfort or annoyance at the way we're straightjacketed by society's expectations of us.

As I'm about to discuss in Chapter 4, inequality and sexism are inextricably linked. They feed off each other. These are not benign forces that, left to their own devices, will atrophy and die out. The opposite is true. Only shining the light of awareness on them can cause them to shrink back or retreat.

It's not men who are deliberately giving us these messages. It's our patriarchal culture, which has evolved over thousands of years, which both men and women perpetuate daily. We soak up these stereotypes, conform to them, and pass them on to the next generation.

Men have their own societal gender straightjackets too: they tell them who they're supposed to be and how they're supposed to behave, and they risk losing their sense of belonging, their identity, or their idea of their manhood if they don't conform to those. But that's a whole other book; our focus here is on how these affect girls and women.

But this leads me to the fact that our current situation is not all men's fault. Women also have to take responsibility for the ways in which we've been blind to, and have perpetuated, these stereotypes. We have to wake up to how things have been, how they still are, and become aware of the part we have played – and how we can do things differently going forward.

When we see the straightjackets, we can't unsee them. When we begin to consider them, we realise that we've taken on board a multitude of these throughout our life. Be curious about how they play out in your life. Start to question them. The things you do to belong, or to be accepted by others, to fit in. It doesn't mean you necessarily have to do anything about them. You don't have to rock any boats or challenge any norms when you become more aware – unless you want to.

Then as you begin to wake up to this stuff, you only need to think about how your life might be if you were to slip out of your straightjacket – or at least loosen it a bit.

CHAPTER 4

Inequality

One of the main consequences of sexist societal programming is inequality. A disparity between the life experiences of men and women. This inequality is often most obvious in the areas where we live most of our lives – in our homes and in the workplace.

As an ambassador for Women's Enterprise Scotland (WES) for eight years, I've become more and more aware of the pervasiveness of, and difficult issues surrounding, both these areas. (Women's Enterprise Scotland is a research-led, not-for-profit, Community Interest Company that champions women-led and women-owned businesses.) Unfortunately, even in the 2020s inequality is alive and well, making the need for organisations such as WES increasingly necessary.

WES, and other organisations in the UK, Europe, the USA and throughout the world, have to fight hard to make the voices of women heard, to push for women to get seats at the tables of power, and to hold to account organisations, governments and individuals responsible for perpetuating outdated, unfair or unjust behaviours, policies, legislation and operational environments and conditions. In other words, those that continue to attempt to get away with treating women as second-class citizens.

Any advances we've seen in the arena of gender equality over the past few decades haven't evolved naturally, or been handed to us on a silver platter; they've nearly always been fought for, often at great personal cost, by brave individuals and organisations who were willing to upset the apple cart and do what was needed to be done to change the status quo. I'll talk about this more in Chapter 9 on feminism.

Not only do these people and organisations still fight for equality but, infuriatingly, they are also often fighting just to hold on to many of the rights that women have already won – although you would think these would be a given by now. Without their tireless work, many of the rights that we have today, and which we should be able to take for granted, could be eroded away or actively taken from us. Terrifying. Unbelievable. But also true.

Inequality in the workplace

It may often seem that women have made great progress in the world of work since the Dark Ages of the 1950s, where women's place was in the home and women's career aspirations were frowned upon or even ridiculed. Although there are now few career paths that are completely inaccessible for women, and women's representation in traditionally male-dominated fields has grown over time, we're still far from an equal playing field when it comes to gender parity in the workplace.

In the UK, Business in the Community's *The Class of 2023 Insights Report* shares insights from *The Times* Top 50 Employers for Gender Equality: 'the UK's most highly profiled and well-established listing of employers taking action to create workplaces where everyone, regardless of gender, can thrive'.[11]

In the report, it's clear that there is still a strong need to focus on gender equality in the workplace. It states that 'despite perceptions, many indicators for gender equality are staying static, or are at risk of sliding backwards' and that 'applying an intersectional lens makes this even more stark: for women from Black, Asian, mixed race and other ethnically diverse backgrounds, inequality has worsened.'[12]

The key areas in which BITC thinks businesses need to be doing more are: disparities in pay and power; persistent issues around women's significant risk of job insecurity; and also women's risk of gender-based harassment and discrimination in the workplace. Here are some eye-opening statistics from the report:

---

11 Business in the Community (12 July 2023), The Class of 2023 Insights Report.
    https://www.bitc.org.uk/report/the-class-of-2023-insights-report/
12 Ibid.

- In the UK, women in employment earn 85p for every pound a man earns. In the US they earn 83 cents for every dollar a man earns.[13] The average for countries in the EU is a slightly 'healthier' 87.3 cents to every euro.[14]
- Women continue to be under-represented in senior positions, currently holding around 31% of senior management roles. Only 6% of CEOs of FTSE 100 companies are women.[15]
- 52% of women say they have experienced bullying and harassment in the workplace: however, very few report it.[16]
- Working women in the UK are nearly twice as likely (1.8 times) as men to be in severely insecure work.[17]

These are some of the stats, but from my own experience and from anecdotal evidence from friends,

---

13 Pew Research Center (1 March 2023), 'Gender pay gap in US hasn't changed much in two decades.' https://www.pewresearch.org/short-reads/2023/03/01/gender-pay-gap-facts/

14 Eurostat Statistics (March 2023), 'Gender pay gap statistics.' https://ec.europa.eu/eurostat/statistics-explained/index.php?title=Gender_pay_gap_statistics

15 Catalyst (1 March 2022), Research: Women in Management (Quick take). https://www.catalyst.org/research/women-in-management/

16 Harriet Minter (2 April 2014), '52% of women have been bullied or harassed at work in the past three years.' The Guardian. https://www.theguardian.com/women-in-leadership/2014/apr/02/52-percent-women-experience-bullying

17 Diversity UK (October 2022), The Gender Gap: Insecure work in the UK. https://diversityuk.org/wp-content/uploads/2022/10/The-Gender-Gap-Report.pdf

family and work colleagues, we know what these statistics can translate into in reality: women being left out of important, relevant meetings by male colleagues; being overlooked for promotion, even though their qualifications are more appropriate for the job than her male counterpart's; marriage or childbirth causing a negative impact on a woman's career opportunities within an organisation (this is usually unspoken); being expected to dress in an overtly feminine way; being asked to carry out more menial tasks than males at a similar level or with similar length of experience are not asked to; being expected to laugh at or at least not mind sexist 'banter'; and being expected to accept being marginalised and treated in many unfair ways, large and small, that male colleagues aren't.

While this still continues in any workplace, to a greater or lesser degree, there is still much work to be done before women are seen as equally capable human beings, deserving of respect. It doesn't seem a lot to ask.

I also want to address something I've come across several times that I'll describe as the 'it's gone too much the other way' brigade. Some people (including some women) seem to think that focusing on making things fairer for girls and women somehow disadvantages boys and men: that putting in place structures, laws or guidelines that require equal representation of males and females is somehow 'taking it too far', and that any bias towards women to try to redress the balance that has been skewed in men's favour since time immemorial is somehow unfair to men.

Well, first, positive, proactive bias towards women is only necessary *because* of the huge bias towards males that there has been for centuries in all spheres of life. I would say that the pendulum needs to swing the other way until women's increased representation in all areas of life is so much the norm that the pendulum will hopefully eventually settle around the middle. But there is a long way to go before that happens.

Many men might feel aggrieved that it seems to be 'all about power for women now'. Well, of course they are. They've had things their own way for so long that it's bound to feel uncomfortable, different, 'wrong' or 'too much the other way'. But it isn't. It's necessary, and long overdue.

Inequality in the home

Where do I start with this? As I mentioned earlier, 1950s stereotypes around gender roles are still alive and well, and are often most apparent when it comes to housework and childcare.

If you're female and everyone in your household, male and female, shares the domestic burden equally, then you are in the minority.

The European Institute for Gender Equality Index of 2021[18] reports that 91% of women with children spend at

---

18 Gender Equality Index 2021. 'Gender differences on household chores.' https://eige.europa.eu/publications-resources/toolkits-guides/gender-equality-index-2021-report/gender-differences-household-chores

least an hour per day on housework, compared with 30% of men with children. It also states that 'entrenched gender roles in terms of housework responsibilities come from parental role models, passing the inequality from one generation to the next'. Their research showed clearly that even adolescent girls and young women do more work in the childhood home than their male counterparts.

Housework, of course, is only one type of unpaid work in a household. There is also childcare, caring for family members with disabilities or chronic health conditions, or caring for elderly relatives. When it comes to childcare, guess what? Women do the majority of this work too. In 2022 in the USA, around 7% of stay-at-home parents were male.[19] In the UK it's slightly higher at 10.6%. Here too the gender roles seem to be ingrained.[20]

Every couple has to choose what suits them best when they have a child. Will one of them stay at home with the child, or will the child go to a nursery from an early age? This might be a difficult decision when both partners work full-time – at least, you might think it is. More often than not, though, it's assumed that the woman will be the main

---

19 G. Livingston and K. Parker (2019), '8 facts about American dads.' Pew Research Center, https://www.pewresearch.org/short-reads/2019/06/12/fathers-day-facts/

20 Fatherhood Institute (January 2023), 'Stay-at-home dads rise by a third since pre-pandemic.' http://www.fatherhoodinstitute.org/2023/stay-at-home-dads-rise-by-a-third-since-pre-pandemic/

carer – even if she plans to go back to work, or she earns more than her partner did before having the baby.

Some women are pushed into the role of full-time parent or main carer, some women feel they don't have much choice about it, and some women take on the role willingly, or even relish the thought of it. Whichever camp you fall into, at some point you'll find out what the reality of staying at home with a child is like – the sheer weight of demands, and the fact that you're expected to meet almost all of those demands. Then, to add insult to injury, the all-consuming, life-sucking, self-denying, juggling act that is being a parent or full-time carer is viewed by society as – at best – 'the easy option' or 'not really work', and at worst it's seen as an option for a woman with no career aspirations, or who's conservative, old-fashioned or possibly even lazy.

Women are relentlessly judged for how we carry out our roles as mothers by everyone – family, friends, the media, teachers, neighbours, sports coaches, etc. It seems that everyone has the right to have an opinion on how we perform that role. Imagine that was the case with other forms of work, if everyone felt free to wade in and tell people all that they were doing wrong, or how they could be doing it better or differently!

Of course, we're also really good at judging *ourselves* too. We have an ingrained idea of how the role *should* be done, and we judge how close we are to that ideal. We're really good at beating ourselves up for not meeting all the standards that society sets for succeeding in the role. The topic of being a mother is a huge one, but I'm trying to stay on track here by talking about equality in our homes. Division of labour. Who does what and why.

As well as doing the majority of the housework, women often shoulder the burdens of grocery shopping, cooking, organising their children's timetables, giving lifts to after-school hobbies and clubs, dealing with school admin and events, arranging their children's social lives, and remembering birthdays and buying presents – as well as an assortment of other life admin tasks. Often all of this can be on top of working part-time or full-time.

Talking of this invisible, unlimited work, experts say that 'this hidden work comes in three overlapping categories: cognitive labour (basically, thinking about everything), emotional labour (maintaining the family emotionally), and the intersection of these two in the mental load of preparing, organising and anticipating everything, emotional and practical, that needs to get done to make life flow.'[21]

How heavily are domestic and/or childcare chores weighted towards you (and possibly other females in your household) compared with the men? Why is that? Start

---

21 Melissa Hogenboom (25 May 2021), 'The gender biases that shape our brains.' https://www.bbc.com/future/article/20210524-the-gender-biases-that-shape-our-brains

noticing where there is an unequal division of domestic labour.

And that might just be the start of it. What about all the other things you do to make the household and everyone's lives run smoothly – do you really need to do *all* of these things? If you're thinking about all these things, a great book to read is *Wifework* by Susan Maushart. [22]

I'm not trying to incite a mutiny here – but feel free if the spirit moves you! – just awareness and understanding. How have we got to this point in our roles and the way we live our lives? Does it feel fair? For me, striving to achieve a more equal sharing of the domestic load, whether this is housework or childcare, isn't just about the principle of equality; it's also about self-care.

The extra hours a woman puts into housework and so on are often the very hours that, if things were shared more equally, she could have for herself, for her own pursuits, to look after herself or have some downtime, for relaxation or fun. This free time will allow her to experience life as a healthier, happier human being – and let's face it, she'll be much better able to tackle the demands of the household and her caring roles after having some downtime. It's a win/win for everybody.

---

22 Bloomsbury Publishing, 2002.

CHAPTER 5

Sexism

In her great book, *Everyday Sexism*, and on her website of the same name,[23] Laura Bates talks about the insidiousness of the widespread sexism that most women deal with throughout their lives. It's a sad state of affairs that we count ourselves as 'fortunate' if the worst of our experiences of sexism, or male violence, have been few or minor, as there can't be many women who *don't* know women who have suffered much more than we have.

Everyday sexism

Girls and women get used to being stared at, being called endearments like 'honey' or 'love' (or often much more sexual terms) by complete strangers, being wolf-whistled at, enduring sexist 'jokes' and 'banter', and hearing boys or men talking about them and/or other women as a collection of body parts, rather than sentient human

---

23   Laura Bates (2015), Everyday Sexism. Simon & Schuster.

beings. The objectification of girls and women is just one type of sexism.

Whether it's in a work setting, socially, in the street, or maybe even in our homes, we all know that we might see or experience sexism on a daily basis. In some circumstances, we might enjoy male attention – such as wolf-whistling – as a boost for our ego, but most of the time it bothers us, especially the more aware we are of how sexist it is: and that it's the thin end of the wedge that leads to worse, more damaging sexist behaviours.

More often than not, though, even when we're bothered by it, we probably say or do nothing. It goes unchallenged. Look at my earlier examples of the things I said nothing about. *Women feel more uncomfortable challenging sexism than putting up with it.* We're used to accepting these experiences as just part of life.

Think about all the instances of everyday sexism that you can remember experiencing. It could be in a work setting, at school, socialising or at home. Try to recall times where you've felt belittled, mocked, that you have been treated unfairly, had to endure sexist remarks or 'jokes', been treated like an idiot, or had to fend off unwanted male attention or male predatory behaviours … simply because you're a woman. It might even be hard for you to remember a lot of this if you've got accustomed to tuning it out.

I hope it won't be upsetting for you to do this. But to me it feels important to do this, because the first step in combatting sexism is being aware of it. You can't deal with something differently, or create a strategy to tackle something, if you don't know what it is. It's by recognising all the incidences of sexism in your life that you begin to see the truth of what you've put up with as a woman. You begin to wake up to how much sexism you have to contend with daily, or have had to deal with in the past.

The type, amount and degree of these experiences will be different for each of us, and will affect each of us differently. I think a good description of this is an analogy that Glennon Doyle used on her 'We Can Do Hard Things' podcast. She likened the sexism and patriarchy that women experience as like constantly inhaling a toxic gas that is in the air we breathe. Some of us are more affected by it than others, while some get more sick with it (which might show up in addictions or other self-destructive outlets), but it affects us all, even if we don't realise it.

The darker side

So, most of us tolerate the everyday sexism that women encounter on a daily basis. What about the slide towards more overt, aggressive, threatening, abusive or violent forms of sexist behaviour? The two tend to be portrayed as separate things, as if there is everyday sexism (catcalling, jokes, objectification and other sexist attitudes) and a separate entity of violence against girls and women (groping, stalking, rape, physical abuse and murder). They are, however, inextricably linked. They are on a continuum. They are all part of the same problem. And we can't turn a blind eye to this link if we've been 'fortunate' enough to have experienced only the less severe forms of sexism. It is a sliding scale that we could all find ourselves on at any point throughout our lives – such is the nature of the beast.

I'm going to use myself as a case study. If I were to discount all the 'commonplace' sexism that I've experienced throughout my life, such as sexist jokes, disrespect due to gender, wolf-whistling, crude remarks, being propositioned, patronised or treated like I was stupid, and seeing women objectified in every area of life, there are still a variety of distressing or disturbing incidents that have occurred throughout my life.

I'm going to list the incidents that stick in my mind because they were scary, threatening or emotionally traumatic. I want to add at this point that I'm 5ft 11in. (1.8m) tall, and have always felt quite strong and capable physically, and I've never felt physically scared by much in life. However, these incidents, even the ones that didn't involve being in physical danger, stand out in my mind because they had a negative impact on me psychologically or emotionally. They made me feel vulnerable, physically or psychologically. They're examples of the type of experiences women have to deal with just because we're women.

Here goes.

- I was about ten or eleven. In the woods behind our house, a boy neighbour (I think a year or two older) made me lie on the grass next to him, lift up my top to show him my chest, and let him touch me. He told me that if I didn't, he would tell everyone that I had let him anyway (how did this little bastard know to blackmail me at this age?). Anyway, not that big a deal, right? But I remember feeling a mix of confusion, shame and humiliation about it. I was scared that someone would find out and that I'd get into trouble: I felt that I must have been doing something wrong to have to keep it secret.

- Fast-forward fourteen years. We'd moved house when I was twelve, so I never saw this boy again until I opened the door of my flat where I lived alone, aged twenty-five, and he was standing there in a police officer's uniform. He said something about working at a police station nearby and seeing my name on something and realising we'd grown up together... I can't remember exactly what he said. Alarm bells were going off in my head and in my body, and I couldn't get rid of him, and shut the door, quickly enough. He seemed puzzled. I really think he'd expected me to welcome him with open arms and invite him in.
- Age twenty, at a party in London, a guy I'd never met before came over to my cousin and I and interrupted our conversation. We were standing against a wall. He put his hands either side of our heads, put his face up close to ours, and said, 'Why don't the two of you come in that bedroom with me? I'll make you both squeal like little pigs!' Eugh! Just eugh! After we refused him, he proceeded to follow us around for the rest of the night, glaring at us. We felt uncomfortable and intimidated, so we left early.

- Earlier, I told you about being pinned against the wall by a man I'd gone out with a few times. This happened to me another time, but in a much scarier situation. I was in my mid-twenties and volunteered with a homeless charity in the evenings, giving soup and sandwiches to rough sleepers on the streets and at bus stations. I wasn't working this night, though. I'd been out with friends at a bar. It was about midnight, and I left to walk back to my flat. The bar was down a lane from the main road. As I walked along the lane, from a recessed doorway a voice said, 'Hello'. It was a young homeless guy I knew from working with the charity. Tall, broad-shouldered. He always seemed a decent guy. I stopped to talk to him, and he came out of the doorway, but over the course of the next few minutes – without me being aware of it happening – I ended up with my back to the doorway, he was closing in on me, and I was stepping back. I realised this too late though. As he lifted his hand towards my neck, he said 'I could just grab you by the throat just now', and he did, pushing me against the door. He wasn't angry; he was playing with me. He wanted to see how I would react. He was like a cat with a mouse. A terrified mouse.

- I could tell by his eyes, now inches away from mine, that he'd been taking drugs. I didn't know what to do, but my survival instinct took over. I said to him really calmly that he didn't want to do this. I didn't try to get away or struggle. I kept smiling. I tried not to let him see I was scared. Time seemed to stand still, and for what seemed like an eternity he kept smiling, squeezing lightly on my neck, and pushing me against the door. Then he let go, stood back and smiled. I calmly said, 'Bye, take care', but when I walked away and got round the corner, I ran like the wind all the way back to my flat. It felt like a lucky escape.

- One of my first jobs was working in Police HQ in Glasgow doing admin in the chief constable's office. On my way to work one morning at 8am, right next to the building where I worked, a guy walked past me and I felt a hand going up my skirt from behind and grabbing my pants under my skirt. I swung round, and he was off and running down the street. Since it happened outside Police HQ, you can imagine the fuss when I went into work. I didn't want to pursue it because I didn't even see the man, just his rear view as he ran away, and I was fine, but they weren't having it. I spent ages looking at mugshots to try to identify him, but of course, I couldn't.

- In my twenties, I was at my parents' hotel on the west coast of Scotland for a weekend, and they had a band playing. The singer in the band was quite attractive and friendly. When the bar closed, we were having a drink and talking. He said about maybe going on a date sometime, but I explained that I had just had a relationship that didn't work out, that I wasn't over that – and anyway, I was about to go backpacking around the world in a few weeks so I wasn't really interested in a relationship.

- We walked through from the bar together, and saw that everyone else had gone to bed. I said goodnight to him. As I started to walk upstairs to my parents' flat within the hotel, he said, 'Lynn, would you like to do something with this?' I turned round. He was standing at the bottom of the stairs, his trousers round his knees, his erect dick in his hand. I couldn't believe it. I didn't feel scared; I was actually trying not to laugh. He started to walk up the stairs towards me, still holding his dick. I just said, 'Sorry, no', and shot off upstairs. I managed to get in the flat door before I burst out laughing: out the corner of my eye, I could see him trying to stuff his penis back into his jeans, but he couldn't get it back in.

- I tell you that story because although that incident wasn't scary or threatening for me (I think because of the setting, and because I knew there were lots of people asleep in bedrooms around us), for someone else it could have been terrifying. It's also an illustration of how entitled some men can be. Even though I had made it clear I wasn't interested, he wasn't taking no for an answer.

- In my thirties, when I was walking along a country road near the farm where we live, a car passed me then pulled over onto the verge a bit ahead of me. A guy got out – youngish, maybe early twenties. I thought he was going to ask for directions, but he took out his dick and started masturbating towards me. I was stunned, but my reaction surprised even myself. I started shouting at him and kept walking towards him, so he jumped back in his car and sped off. All the while I was still shouting at him, then running after the car and shaking my fist! (I can't even remember what I was shouting. It would be good if it had been 'Don't wank at me!')

These are just the things that I can remember. There are probably more, and most of these are quite tame compared to what many women have experienced. I feel very fortunate never to have had to fend off anyone sexually, or put up with the overt predatory behaviours that many girls and women have to deal with today. It seems that this is particularly common today – more common than it used to be?

So, somewhere on the continuum between everyday sexism and violence/sexual violence, there are the disturbing, destructive or damaging experiences. We tolerate because 'they weren't that bad', or we keep quiet, out of fear that if we do speak up we'll be told that we're over-reacting, that we need to 'lighten up', that 'boys will be boys', or that somehow we were at fault. We don't get taken seriously: in our concerns, our experiences or the effect they have on us. Unless we have experienced violence or sexual violence, our experiences are dismissed as 'that's just what life is like for a woman' – and we get into the habit of accepting this.

But accepting, ignoring or tolerating 'lesser' types of sexism, aggression or boundary-pushing creates fertile ground in which the seeds of stalking, sexual violence, domestic violence or murder grow and thrive.

The figure below illustrates how the small things that seem not worth causing a fuss about accumulate and create a toxic environment where instances of sexism, abuse, inequality, injustice and inhumanity against women and girls increase and get more serious.

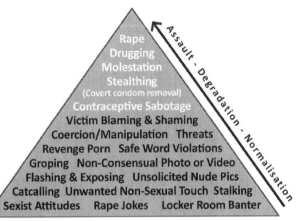

Tolerance of the behaviours at the bottom supports or excuses
those higher up. To change outcomes, we must change the culture

Figure: The rape culture pyramid. (Source: Version 5.
Created by Jaime Chandra & Cervix. © September 2018.)

By speaking up more, accepting less and tolerating
less, over and over, day by day, we're sprinkling
weedkiller on these sprouting seeds of sexism and male
violence. Believe me, that's enough. It's enough when
enough of us do it, repeatedly.

Violence against women and girls

In this book I talk mainly about Western culture and
society, particularly relating to the ways in which we were
conditioned when we grew up, but when it comes to
violence against women and girls, there is no part of the
world where we're safe.

Estimates published by the World Health Organization in 2021[24] indicate that globally 'about 30% of women worldwide have been subjected to either physical and/or sexual intimate partner violence or non-partner sexual violence in their lifetime'. However, when I was researching this, I noticed that most organisations state that figures are likely to be a lot higher than published: many women don't report incidents due to a fear of retribution, or not believing that justice will be served because of the shockingly low rates of prosecution and conviction of sex offenders.[25] So the statistics, however bad they are, don't even show the full picture. And they are bad.

- In the USA, an average of three women are killed every day.[26] 92% of these are killed by a man they know.[27]

---

24 World Health Organization (9 March 2021), Fact sheet: Violence against women. https://www.who.int/news-room/fact-sheets/detail/violence-against-women

25 Dame Vera Baird (2022), 'The distressing truth is that if you are raped in Britain today, your chances of seeing justice are slim.' Victims Commissioner. https://victimscommissioner.org.uk/news/the-distressing-truth-is-that-if-you-are-raped-in-britain-today-your-chances-of-seeing-justice-are-slim/

26 Sanctuary For Families (10 March 2022), 'The silent epidemic of femicide in the United States.' https://sanctuaryforfamilies.org/femicide-epidemic/

27 Centers for Injury Prevention and Control (2021), National Intimate Partner and Sexual Violence Survey. https://www.cdc.gov/violenceprevention/datasources/nisvs/index.html

- On average, two women are killed each week in the UK by a current or former partner.
- 25% of women in the UK will experience domestic abuse in their lifetime. Only around a quarter of those who do are likely to seek any help, or report it.
- In the USA, 19% of all domestic physical violence involves a weapon.[28]
- 41% of girls in the UK aged 14 to 17 have experienced some form of sexual violence in an intimate relationship.[29]
- In the USA, 18.3% of women reported having been raped or sexually abused.[30]
- In the UK in 2022, nearly 70% of rape survivors withdrew from the justice system, due to low conviction rates and fear of having to relive the trauma in court.[31]

---

28 National Coalition Against Domestic Violence. National Statistics. https://ncadv.org/STATISTICS

29 'What is domestic abuse? The facts.' https://refuge.org.uk/what-is-domestic-abuse/the-facts/

30 https://www.cdc.gov/violenceprevention/datasources/nisvs/index.html

31 Rajeev Syal (30 May 2023), 'Nearly 70% of rape victims drop out of investigations in England and Wales.' https://www.theguardian.com/society/2023/may/30/nearly-70-of-victims-drop-out-of-investigations-in-england-and-wales

- In the USA, 1 in 6 women have experienced stalking, and about 68% of victims experienced threats of physical harm.[32]
- In the UK, data shows that in 2021–22, only 5% of reported stalking cases resulted in a charge, and 2% of reports resulted in a conviction.[33]

(Although men and boys also suffer from sex-based abuse and violence, women and girls are hugely disproportionately affected.)

The above statistics merely give an overview of the scope and scale of the problem. What they *don't* convey is the physical, emotional and psychological harm and damage that is inflicted on girls and women throughout the world, every minute of every day, or the trauma they're left to deal with, often for the rest of their lives.

Statistics don't illustrate the often-heartbreaking individual human stories behind these numbers. The ongoing fear, panic attacks and illnesses that women and girls can be left with as a result of their experiences. The cost to their self-esteem, trust in others, ability to form relationships, often even their ability to work, or even to lead a relatively normal life.

---

32 National Sexual Violence Resource Center (2010), Statistics In-Depth.
    https://www.nsvrc.org/statistics/statistics-depth
33 Suzy Lamplugh Trust, 'An advocate for every victim.'
    https://www.suzylamplugh.org/an-advocate-for-every-victim-independent-stalking-advocates-isas-in-the-victim-and-prisoners-bill

Violence against women and girls is about power and dominance. It's about all the things that have been instilled into men by our patriarchal society. It's the thick end of the wedge that runs from traditional gender roles, ingrained clichés, stereotypes and sexist jokes to their destructive, and often deadly, consequences.

Fundamentally, it's about women and girls not being treated with the dignity that every human being deserves to be treated with, regardless of their sex. It's about not being treated with respect. It's about not being accepted or acknowledged for all that we are as human beings, all that we want to be, and all we want to do and experience in our lives, regardless of our sex.

We just want to be able to live our lives free from the threats of sexism, misogyny and male violence. They are soul-destroying and pervasive, and contribute to destroying and negating our humanity. Work, career, relationships, how you look – all come second to our most basic need to be treated with dignity and respect.

Various high-profile cases have received a lot of media attention, highlighting the abuse of power against women. Two examples are former police constable and firearms officer Wayne Couzens, who was convicted of the kidnapping, rape and murder of Sarah Everard in London in March 2021, and former Hollywood producer Harvey Weinstein, who in 2020 was sentenced to 23 years in prison after being convicted of multiple offences of sexual assault and rape.

These have triggered waves of women's voices detailing the sexist attitudes and behaviours that you and

I, and every woman, meets throughout her life, and has to put up with on a daily basis. Alongside this, others have felt able to open up about their traumatic experiences of violence or abuse, rape, stalking, intimidation, blackmail … the list goes on.

Each and every one of us can make a difference. If we keep doing what we've always done, nothing will change. Every time we notice even a mildly sexist attitude or comment, and let it go, it's like leaving a cancerous cell intact. Every time we tolerate a sexist joke or stay silent in the face of sexist behaviour, it's like feeding a group of cancerous cells. Make no mistake: these cells multiply and become the tumours in our society that are porn culture, domestic violence, stalking, rape and murder.

CHAPTER 6

The crisis in schools

As I mentioned in the introduction, I started writing this book after I read a shocking article in *The Times* one Sunday morning. At the time, if I had been asked where I thought we were, as a culture, in dealing with sexism and the patriarchy, I would probably have said that although women still have some way to go to achieve equal rights, at least young women and girls weren't experiencing as much sexism as I grew up with in the 80s and 90s. I thought that at least girls were being treated by boys more as equals now – in general. So, when I read the article, I had a very rude awakening.

This article talked about the porn, rape and abuse culture that permeates secondary schools, creating a toxic environment for girls (and boys). As the mother of a girl who had just turned thirteen and had just started secondary school, I was horrified at what I was reading. It sickened me and chilled me to the bone – not only as a mother, but also as a woman. In horrific detail, the article outlined the ways in which at many, many schools, girls were being treated in the following ways:

- Openly rated by boys for their breasts, bums, legs and lips (good or bad for blow jobs). These ratings were then posted on social media or in school chat groups.
- Boys constantly trying to take photos up girls' skirts (upskirting) or in changing rooms to post on chat groups or social media.
- Girls encouraged, and pressurised, by boys they were going out with to take intimate pictures of themselves, then – humiliatingly – the boys shared these photos in various online groups.
- Girls being casually groped in school corridors and in the playground; this was dismissed as banter.
- Boys targeting drunk girls at parties and taking naked photos of them or even raping them, then joking about it and openly talking about it, because they didn't see it as rape. The girls were their 'friends', and they were 'out of their face', so 'it didn't count as rape'!

This article was borne out of testimonies on a site called Everyone's Invited.[34] Soma Sara, a young woman who'd had enough of being on the receiving end of predatory, sexist behaviour at university, talked to some friends about it and was surprised by the commonality of their experiences. In June 2020 she decided to create a website to allow others to post their experiences, and soon a tsunami of girls – and some boys – posted their stories on the site. The testimonies are anonymous, but each

---

34 https://www.everyonesinvited.uk/

person who leaves a story gives the name of their school, college or university.

In 2021, the number of schools represented on this website grew and grew, as did the number of testimonies. At the time of writing this (early 2023), there are over 50,000 testimonies.

This website and the publicity it generated prompted an Ofsted investigation (Ofsted is the UK government department responsible for inspecting and monitoring a range of educational institutions, including schools). The results were published in June 2021, with Ofsted reporting that:

Sexual harassment and online sexual abuse are so routine for schoolchildren that they barely bother reporting it; 90% of girls and 50% of boys have been sent explicit pictures. Girls, the biggest targets of harassment, report everything from unwanted touching, rape jokes and upskirting to being asked for nude images and having nudes shared on Snapchat and WhatsApp 'like a collection game'.[35]

Ofsted chief inspector Amanda Spielman said she was 'shocked' by the findings. She also said: 'It's alarming that many children and young people, particularly girls, feel they have to accept sexual harassment as part of

---

35 Ofsted (10 June 2021), Review of sexual abuse in schools and colleges. https://www.gov.uk/government/publications/review-of-sexual-abuse-in-schools-and-colleges

growing up.' At every school Ofsted visited young people reported a significant problem: 'It wasn't in some, *it was in all of them*,' she said.

She went on to say that: 'Whether it's happening at school or in their social life, they simply don't feel it's worth reporting. This is a cultural issue – it's about attitudes and behaviours becoming normalised, and schools and colleges can't solve that by themselves.'

I hope that you're as disturbed by reading this as I was. It's clear that there is currently a toxic environment in schools, colleges and universities that is not conducive to girls and young women (and boys and young men) being able to make the most of their educational opportunities or learn about healthy adult relationships.

Young adults and porn

Reading that article reminded me of an article I'd read a couple of years ago on the BBC which also really bothered me at the time. It was about female university students speaking out about men's expectations in sexual relationships. They said that they regularly experienced men looking to recreate scenes they had watched in online porn, often of extremely aggressive or rough sex, sometimes including strangulation or simulating violence. Several young women were interviewed for the article, all in their final year at university, and they all said that they had encountered this tendency in 'most of' the relationships they'd had over the past few years.

The young women also said that, when they had been reluctant to participate in aggressive sex, their boyfriends had made them feel that they were being 'unsexy', 'uncool' or 'frigid', or had said that 'other girls are into it', implying there was something wrong with them if they weren't.

What the hell! Why is sexual harassment so normalised in our society that girls and young women don't even bother to speak about it to anyone, as it's just expected? Why do they accept that nothing is likely to be done about it?

What has online porn done to our boys? What is it doing to their brains that many of them are treating girls so appallingly? What is experiencing this kind of behaviour doing to our girls? How does it affect their learning and schoolwork or university work? How does this affect them physically, mentally, emotionally and spiritually? What does it do for their sense of their own humanity? How will it affect their long-term romantic relationships?

Most teenage boys (and some girls), whether through actively searching for porn or through peer pressure, will have seen online porn – and the most soulless, unsexy, dehumanising, mechanical versions of sex, lacking in any intimacy or passion. In porn, sex is also often degrading, humiliating, aggressive or violent for the woman, or women, involved. And of course, the women will be looking as if they're loving it; alternatively, they might be resisting – until they either give in or are overpowered.

This is what's being programmed into the minds of teenage boys – and often before they've even kissed a girl. Porn can normalise harmful, abusive, or violent behaviour, and affect the emotional and psychological development of everyone who watches it.

Long gone are the days when pornography came in the form of 'dirty magazines' that a boy kept well hidden in his bedroom. Now, porn streams onto their phone wherever they are. They can be watching it at school, on the bus, in their bedroom, in the bathroom: straight from their phone and into their psyche and into their souls. Their brains are being programmed to think that this is what sex is. That this is what women want. Porn is fuelling their fantasies and imagination of what sex ought to be like – which isn't going to be much fun for the poor girl they have real-life sex with.

Maybe, though, some boys instinctively know that watching porn doesn't seem right. Maybe it makes them feel 'bad', or that they're doing something wrong by watching it, and then they feel ashamed of themselves. Their sexual desires might instead become attached to feelings of shame, guilt and low self-esteem, which can lead to other problems in their relationships with women.

Either way, there is no happy ending for teenage boys who become addicted to watching the type of porn that is readily available online – and being targeted at the younger generation. The ease with which young boys – some as young as eight or nine – can view pornography, and the nature of the porn, is recognised as being a huge contributory factor in the current culture of sexism in schools. Yet a new age-verification law, announced by the UK government, due to come into force in 2019, which would require all pornography websites to verify that users were over eighteen, was abandoned after years of work by various organisations.[36] It would have been groundbreaking, and the UK would have been the first country in the world to protect under-18s in this way. It is hoped that the UK government's new Online Safety Bill, currently making its way through Parliament, will resurrect this age-verification requirement.

The effects of porn on girls

A study published in the *Journal of Adolescent Health* found that sexual harassment against girls aged thirteen and fourteen was 'associated with elevated risk of self-harm, suicidal thoughts, maladaptive dieting, early dating, substance use and feeling unsafe at school'.[37] The study concluded that greater efforts at prevention and intervention are needed to address this.

---

36 UK Government (21 September 2023), Online Safety Bill.
   https://bills.parliament.uk/bills/3137
37 D. Chiodo et al. (2009), 'Impact of sexual harassment victimization by peers on subsequent adolescent victimization and adjustment: a longitudinal study.' The Journal of Adolescent Health 45(3), 246–252. https://doi.org/10.1016/j.jadohealth.2009.01.006

Another study, 'Sexual harassment and the developing sense of self among adolescent girls',[38] had the aim of detecting the effects of sexual harassment on girls' well-being and 'developing sense of self'. It went on to say that the rhetoric of '"boys will be boys" is a phenomenon that cripples girls, boys and their relations with themselves, others and the world'.

The study also stated that 'The negation and trivialisation of girls' experiences, and their diminishing sense of selves, appears to be intensified by inappropriate responses on the part of trusted adults in whom the girls confide.'

So, not only does our culture trivialise the experiences of young girls and pressurise them to adhere to societal programming, hugely affecting the way their sense of self develops, but when girls experience sexual harassment or abuse, the study stated that there was usually a 'lack of responsiveness by significant adults'. Of course, this is likely to further damage the girls emotionally and psychologically, as well as damaging their sense of self.

This is how girls learn to discount their own instincts, their own judgement around what feels right or wrong for them and their bodies. Their sense of self is bound up in

---

38 H. Berman et al. (2007), 'Sexual harassment and the developing sense of
    self among adolescent girls.' Canadian Journal of Counselling and
    Psychotherapy 36(4). Retrieved from https://cjc-
    rcc.ucalgary.ca/article/view/58698

what others think of them, as well as in how well they conform to their societal programming.

Shockingly, this study was conducted nearly twenty years ago: since then, things seem to have got worse rather than better. Today, article after article, news programme after news programme, tell us that girls and young women in our culture are experiencing toxic, damaging sexual harassment at school, college and university, on the streets, at parties with friends, at bars and in clubs. And still they don't speak up because this harassment is so frequent and commonplace that girls are expected to tolerate it. They see no point in speaking up. They believe, often rightly, that nothing would be done if they did speak up, and that they might also face retribution or shaming.

It's a mess. If things to be so awful in male/female relationships at the teens into twenties stage, what will happen when these age groups are then setting up homes, getting married, having families and creating a future together? If all these articles are correct about how widespread sexism and vile attitudes towards woman are, then how do men's fractured, abusive attitudes towards girls and women become healthier all of a sudden? As a boy matures, is he likely to suddenly see girls and women in a different light?

Tackling the teen crisis

So, what can *we* do about this? Eradicating access to online porn for everyone aged under twenty-one would be a good start. In the absence of this, things will only change if the messages that boys and girls are being programmed with change: only if they are educated about societal programming, sexism, gender stereotypes and about treating people, whatever their sex, with humanity and respect, as well as being educated about biology, the mechanics of sexual intercourse, and contraception. They will only change if parents, carers, wider family, schools, colleges, universities and employers make a concerted effort to change things, and if the establishments where young people socialise do the same.

It starts with each one of us modelling zero tolerance of everyday sexist attitudes, behaviours and incidents. It starts with nipping these in the bud and calling them out. We have the opportunity to talk to our children. Kids get sex education at school. But what are they being taught? Is their school teaching them about respect for other human beings, and the continuation of this into sexual relationships? Is their school teaching them to have respect for their own bodies, and for the bodies of others? If not, why not?

Many schools are becoming more proactive at addressing subjects such as consent, sexist language, sexual harassment, online dangers and the rhetoric of misogynistic online influencers, which is great, but this seems to be very ad hoc. Our children's schools will tell us what subjects they are addressing, and with which age groups – we only need to ask.

And if your school won't give your children this information, will you? If not, why not? Because it would make you uncomfortable? Because your child would be uncomfortable/would tell you to get lost/wouldn't listen? With something so serious, are we really willing to make excuses and put our own discomfort, or anxiety about making our child uncomfortable, above the damage that could be done to them if they are a boy watching porn or a girl interacting with boys who are watching porn. And let's face it: if you have a teenage son or daughter, there is a high chance that they will fall into one of these categories.

Having difficult conversations

When my son was eleven or twelve, I needed to talk to him, and I seized my moment one day when I passed him on the stairs of our house. I made him sit on the top step with me. I'd had some stuff brewing inside me for months that I wanted to say to him. I hadn't planned or rehearsed it, and it went something like this.

Me: 'I need to talk to you about some stuff that you're probably not going to want to hear me talk about.'

Him: Puzzled look.

Me: You don't need to say anything, but you can if you want, but I need you to listen though, and you need to nod your head to let me know that you understand what I'm saying. Okay?'

Him: Looks worried, but silently nods his head.

Me: 'You're getting to an age now where you are going to be starting to look at girls in a different way than maybe you have in the past.'

(He rolled his eyes and groaned because he knew what was coming. He got up to go.)

Me: 'No, you need to listen to this. I'm not going to say much, and I know you don't like it, but I need to say it.'

I proceeded to talk to him about relationships between boys and girls, about respect for himself and others, about consent, the law, condoms, sex – he got the works!

He sat there the whole time, visibly wincing, ready to get up. He did nod a couple of times, but he didn't say a word, and we didn't mention it again until years later. That exchange was about ten years ago, but I remember it as if it was yesterday. I'm so glad I got it out, even though I was also squirming as I delivered my monologue. It wasn't comfortable, but it felt necessary. In hindsight, I wish I'd also said something about online porn, but it wasn't as prolific then and I didn't know much about it.

If you're wondering how you could broach the subject of porn with your son or daughter, you could google for a recent news article about teen porn usage, then mention it to them. You could ask them what they know about it, or discuss what you've been reading about it in this book. Then use that as a conversation starter. You could get your partner/husband to bring up the subject if they're more comfortable speaking to your son or daughter about these things. I think it's just as important for girls to be aware of the facts as boys.

You – and your teen – might find it easier to talk when it's just the two of you, not you and your partner together.

Choose your time: when you're getting on well and your son seems relaxed, and he's not about to go somewhere. Actually, chatting on a car journey can be good: he can't go anywhere, and he doesn't need to look you in the eye!

You don't have to know if your teen watches porn, or how much; they're likely to clam up completely if you go down that road, but it's helpful to talk in general terms about stats and consequences.

With your daughter it might be easier – or it might not – but it's important that you impart the information, for their own good. You might start by asking them if they realise how easily teenage boys can access online porn, and say that it's more violent and extreme than it used to be. Tell them how porn imprints on those who watch it subconscious negative messages about women that can be destructive to their relationships for the rest of their lives.

Hopefully they might then be open to having a conversation with you, depending on their age, about any evidence of a toxic culture at their school, or if they have any concerns or experiences that they want to share. If not, you could finish up by talking to her about having the confidence to stand up for herself, not to put up with being treated badly by a boy, and not to allow herself to be coerced into anything that doesn't feel right. To go with her gut instincts. To respect herself and her body. If a boy doesn't respect her choices, then he's not worth bothering about. You get my drift.

This is all stuff we should have been told when we were young, and we might have made very different choices if we had. I know that I would have done many things differently if I'd had this kind of talk from my parents, but those were different days. We live and learn.

The key thing is that our sons and our daughters, or the boys and the girls in our lives, have the information. That they know what's going on. That they know that there is serious damage happening to teenage boys that's being swept under the carpet. You need to convey to them that porn is damaging: it is affecting the wiring of boys' malleable brains, and their attitudes towards girls and women, and it is affecting their lives and future by dehumanising an aspect of intimate relationships.

The trouble that this will cause in the future is still to be seen, but the trouble it's causing now is evident. As a society, we have to do our bit to raise awareness of porn, to ask ourselves if we're going to let it go unchecked. Are we going to let porn ruin the lives of any more teenage boys and girls?

There's nothing wrong with wanting to avoid difficult conversations. It's human nature. We like our comfort zones; we don't like feeling uncomfortable, awkward, or uneasy, especially if we've initiated a conversation. And these subjects certainly have the potential to make us squirm. But we can't bury our heads in the sand and kid ourselves that our children won't be aware of porn, that it won't affect their lives. If they're a teen living in the Western world, that's highly unlikely.

CHAPTER 7

The blame game
– is it all men's fault?

My husband probably thinks that my answer to the above question would be 'yes', but it isn't. It might seem obvious that men are 'to blame' when it comes to sexism, as they're usually the perpetrators of it: that they are at fault and they just need to change their behaviour. But are they? Is it all men, most men, or just some men? Are all men sexist? What makes some more sexist than others? Are your brothers, sons, dads or husbands sexist? Is the insidious sexism that is all around us all their fault?

I'm not going to say that this is all men's fault for two reasons. The second I'll address in the next chapter, but the first is that boys and men have been indoctrinated into a sexist, patriarchal culture since they were born, the same as we have. They've just been programmed with different sexist messages, to think and feel that they're the superior sex, and have soaked it up in the same way that we have our programming. But their messaging has been in their *favour*, as opposed to ours being detrimental to us. But they ignore this, because there is no benefit to them in seeing it and losing their advantages.

On the most seemingly benign level, boys and men have become accustomed to the fact that men will often monopolise mixed-gender conversations, or routinely interrupt and talk over women, and will happily launch into a monologue about a topic, with little regard for whether or not anybody is actually interested in what he has to say. Then there's 'mansplaining', a newish term to describe something that many men have done for a long time: talk down to women condescendingly, or as if they're stupid.

Most men won't be consciously aware of this sense of superiority; it's invisible to them. Of course, they don't have to follow their programming or act on those messages; that's no excuse for sexist attitudes and behaviours, but it all comes back to the cognitive dissonance I talked about before. They may hear new information, but unless they are aware of how this is bumping up against their ingrained programming, there will be a disconnect, and their programming is likely to win.

So, it's too simplistic to solely blame men. Of course, they have to take responsibility for their part in perpetuating sexism, and for their behaviours and actions. They can also influence other men by what they say and how they behave, but that's only part of the solution. To put the responsibility for our still-sexist culture totally at their feet to deal with, to say to them 'this is the way it is, we're not having it any more, do something about it' and step back, isn't going to work, unless they look at the root of their behaviours and attitudes: their societal programming. As I discuss in Chapter 8, women also need to look at their complicity in perpetuating this programming.

We lose an opportunity to take a holistic approach to the problems we face in this arena by expecting men to solve it. Women and men need to tackle this together. We all need to wake up, gain some knowledge and understanding and, with that awareness, begin to do things differently. We *all* need to take responsibility to do whatever we can to make our culture a safer, healthier, more humane place for us all and for future generations.

It'll take a few generations for new behaviours and attitudes to become the norm, and I hope they will, but this will only happen if there is collective awareness, collective responsibility and the collective will to do things differently.

And crucially, men who see this and who are willing to take responsibility to try to change things must be willing to call out the attitudes and behaviours of the men who don't. Too often, the overt sexist behaviours of the minority of men go unchecked because they're condoned by the silence of the majority of men, who know those behaviours are wrong, but say or do nothing.

Their silence isn't benign.

The challenge

Why, in the face of all the public outrage around sexist behaviours these days, do many men not see it, not get it?

Men have always been, on average, larger and physically stronger than women.[39] They *usually* have a larger frame with more muscle tissue, and are taller. How much does that give them a sense of being a more powerful or a superior human being? I'm not saying that they are, or that men consciously think that. But to what degree is this attitude infusing their psyche? In every area of life, we've seen men's physical strength and stature equated with dominance, power and superiority.

Until a few years ago, almost every world leader was male, and most of our governments were made up of men. It's only recently that coverage of professional women's sports has crept into what was almost exclusively a male domain. In most institutions and organisations, it's only recently that women have been more represented – and we still haven't reached parity of representation. It would be very unusual for a male child in the Western world *not* to grow up having his sense of male dominance and superiority enforced and strengthened every day.

The same thing happens to our girls, though. They are also being programmed with the same messages about

---

39 Fair Play For Women (7 July 2017), 'Biological Sex Differences: bones and muscles.' https://fairplayforwomen.com/sex/page/2/

male superiority. We're marinating in the same societal soup as boys, and absorbing all the same messages.

We programme our boys to be boys, and all the history that goes with that, and we programme our girls to be girls, with all the history that goes with that, and then we wonder why little changes in the arena of gender equality.

I remember realising when my son was about ten that, although I chatted to him about girls and women being equal to boys and men and just as capable of doing anything, I was a full-time mum at the time, so what he saw was me cooking, cleaning, shopping, doing the school run, etc. Meanwhile he saw his dad working, and coming home to his dinner ready for him, doing next to no housework and very little childcare.

I realised that this might be what my son would expect when he got married, and it might cause problems in his relationship if his partner had her own career. I could see that this expectation was being programmed into him: that it was the 'norm' for woman to do all the domestic stuff and for the man to go out to work – just as I'd seen my parents do, and just as my husband's parents had done.

My children have since seen me starting a business, and a social enterprise, and writing books, but how much will those affect their ingrained messages?

There's nothing wrong with being a full-time mum; what I'm talking about is being aware of society's messaging and actively trying to counterbalance it. I think that the traditional roles tend to reinforce this messaging rather than challenge it. So it's about being aware of that, and addressing it.

The power struggle

I've introduced the potential subconscious attitudes around superiority and power that a boy or man might have. These are what make some men feel threatened when they see women ascending to positions of power, when they hear how women are taking over the world, or when they hear of various equality initiatives. What does their subconscious brain want men to do when it feels threatened? It wants them to show strength, to dominate, to show power, to exert their superiority.

Male violence against women is a blatant, obvious display of this physical dominance and power – aggression, the impulse to harm, demean, put someone in their place, show your superiority over them – and sexism is the same, just usually less severe or obvious. Sexism and violence against women aren't about sex, they're about power. They're about dominating the other, or ridiculing or demeaning them. It's about putting someone down based on their sex, based on them not being male. It's about making someone a joke because of their sex. It's about devaluing them so that you feel better about yourself. It's about making your sex the superior one. Everyday sexism might be seen as a more 'socially acceptable' form of expressing the messaging from the dominant male psyche than physical violence, but it's still an outlet for expressing dominance. (Remember the Rape Culture figure earlier in this book.)

And now a new outlet for this, especially for younger generations, is how online porn leads to aggression and violence in sexual relationships for teens and young people. Boys' brains are getting wired with destructive, toxic images of girls and women as silent 'dolls' to be treated violently. They are seeing girls and women violated, humiliated and degraded. Pornography is teaching boys that sex is about instant sexual gratification, not intimacy or connection. It's teaching them that sex is all about *them*: what they want, their pleasure. Also, that sex is often about coercion and domination. And boys then take all this into their relationships with girls and, later, women.

Sex, as one of our most animalistic behaviours, is a way for men to act out how they feel about women being a threat to male superiority. Is this why, instead of sexism and violence against women reducing, it's increasing? Is this why, horrifically, the phrase 'nudes, porn, abuse – the toxic culture in UK classrooms' is being used to describe our *schools*? Is it that, as there is more focus on women's equality in various arenas, men are watching violent sex or having violent sex instead of being violent?

Maybe, as there are fewer outlets where they can be openly sexist, and since men are being called out more for violence against women, they turn towards sexual violence as a kind of covert sexism. *But why do they need these outlets?* How can men become less sexist and feel less threatened instead?

Brain rewiring!

A man, understanding about the societal programming of our brains since birth, can see the drive for power and domination this creates in him, and that his mind translates these into feelings of superiority. He can then see that there's not something inherently 'wrong' with him, or with other men, that has caused them to feel conflicted about equality and resist change. He can understand that although his rational brain thinks that of course men and women are equal, and women are just as capable, if he's had a lifetime of seeing male superiority acted out around him and heard about it happening historically for centuries, the difference between what he consciously knows to be true bumps up against what has been programmed into him. Once again, cognitive dissonance.

These mixed messages create uncomfortable feelings, and these uncomfortable feelings urge him to choose to discount the new information and stick with his old beliefs. *However*, when he is aware of this, he can choose to find ways to reinforce the new information and override his subconscious beliefs (more on this in Chapter 11).

By recognising his programming, he realises that he can consciously change that programming: he has a choice. He can choose to create new beliefs, which create new neural pathways in the brain, which in turn create new behaviours. This isn't difficult; we all do it all the time. We do it when we successfully give up a 'bad' habit or practise a new one, and we do it if we learn a new skill.

More and more has been discovered in recent years about how we all – male and female – have the ability throughout our lives to rewire our brains. This is called neuroplasticity. It just means that the old pathways (ingrained thought patterns, attitudes and behaviours) can be changed, however entrenched they are. The only thing that needs to happen is that somebody *wants* to change. Perhaps they know that something isn't the way it should be, maybe they want things to be different for their children, or they have a different perspective on things from gaining new information.

So, with this understanding, men can lower the cognitive dissonance that the healthier message of women's equality might create in them by waking up to their programming and beginning to notice attitudes in themselves that they might feel are wrong or are ashamed of. They can see that they are not bad human beings; they have just been blind to their programming. Then they are far less likely to feel challenged or threatened by women.

Of course, this is presupposing that men are willing to create change, to see the value in understanding why things are the way they are, and why they need to change. Men who are open to seeing men from a new perspective have the opportunity to become women's allies.

This would only be a start: the foundation on which further change could happen, where men could help to address the attitudes and behaviours of other men, and stand shoulder to shoulder with women in making the world a safer, more pleasant place for women and girls to live in. Some men already are.

There are some brilliant books out there. I recommend Lewis Howes' *The Mask of Masculinity*[40] and Mark Greene's *The Little #MeToo Book For Men*[41]. There are also podcasts and social media accounts aimed at deconstructing societal programming around masculinity (man-box culture), and male stereotypes: organisations MenEngage and the Good Men Project, the podcasts 'Now and Men' and 'The Gender Knot', and the hilarious satirical Twitter account @manwhohasitall – which switches the genders when discussing men and women.

They inform and enlighten, and can help men and boys see that there are other options than blindly following their conditioning. These can help men and boys to understand the issues around sexism and misogyny, and how patriarchal conditioning affects both them and women. Engaging with such dialogues also offers men the opportunity to understand themselves better, and to feel better about themselves for wanting to take responsibility for changing their behaviour rather than feeling blamed and shamed into doing so.

There are also organisations led by men – such as MenEngage and the Good Men Project – that campaign to change cultural sexist attitudes and behaviours. They want to work with men and women to

---

40   Lewis Howes (2017), The Mask of Masculinity. Hay House.
41   Mark Greene (2018), The Little #MeToo Book for Men. ThinkPlay Partners.

create change. Women are mothers, daughters, sisters, friends, wives, co-workers – so we have plenty of opportunities to feed new information to others, including men, to give them the chance to gain a different perspective on things.

You could make a start by letting the men in your life read this chapter – or even the whole book!

There are no guarantees that enough men will change to make a difference, but what's the alternative? If they do nothing, if we do nothing, then things definitely won't get better: for ourselves, for the girls and women around us, or for future generations of girls who are growing up in a climate of sexism and sexual violence that no human being deserves to experience. Do men want their daughters, granddaughters, nieces and so on to grow up in such a culture, as well as younger generations of boys, whose lives are also negatively affected by our current culture?

CHAPTER 8

Women's culpability in perpetuating sexism

The second reason that I don't think sexism is all men's fault is because I believe that women are partly to blame for perpetuating our sexist, patriarchal culture. Where might our culpability lie? As an example, think about your mother (and here I want to emphasise that I'm talking about mothers who had no fear of domestic violence from their husbands): did she say anything when you were confronted daily by Page 3 girls in newspapers? If not, didn't she let you down? Every time she heard a sexist joke or comment, what did she do? If she said nothing, or even laughed, wasn't she letting you down? We condone sexism with our silence. We show our children that they're supposed to stay silent about it too, and just put up with it.

Don't get me wrong, I understand why we don't say anything, and why our mothers didn't. I remember attending events over the past few years, when a man has made a sexist joke or comment. I didn't say anything, and I felt bad about myself. I might not have laughed. But I stayed silent. I might have shaken my head, or looked away, or walked away, depending on how sexist or crude it was. I watched other people to see what they did: usually, all the other men laughed and the women's reactions varied from laughing, to smiling, to shaking their heads or just looking uncomfortable. Why, as a grown woman, mother of a daughter, well aware of the insidiousness and destructiveness caused by the perpetuation of sexism, did I not say anything? Maybe I didn't want to 'dampen the mood of the party', be made to feel like a 'man-hater' or risk being told I was 'a bore' or 'a bitch'. And I'm sure I'm not alone in feeling like this.

I could simply have said 'I don't find that funny' or 'Do you realise that's sexist?' or 'That's sexist, so not appropriate' or 'Sexist jokes aren't funny'. There was no need for me to be angry or aggressive about it. It's harder for someone to take offence if you just state the facts and how you feel calmly and firmly, then see what the reaction is. Although these kind of situations happen less and less these days, and it's usually older men who do it. I tend to think I'm letting them off the hook because they don't know any better, but I'm done with that. They ought to know better.

This is why nothing seems to have changed much in many respects, or even if it has outwardly to some degree – because it's not politically correct to say certain things – the undercurrent of old attitudes is still there.

I began to write this book thinking that it was going to be about how women could wake up to how sexist society still is, how we could help men to see this, and how we could together find a way forward for the sake of our children. I presumed that the problem lay with men, but smugly thought that women could be supportive, and magnanimous, in helping them to see the light.

However, here's the sting: most women have also perpetuated sexism and gender inequality, even at the same time as they fight it. We've brought up boys differently from girls. We've unquestioningly perpetuated the gender roles we saw our parents enact, or bought into males' superiority by feeding their egos. You may be one of the women who has never done this, and if so, that's brilliant, but there aren't many of you.

An eye-opener for me about this was a United Nations report I read recently, which was published in March 2020.[42] The Gender Social Norms Index measures how social beliefs obstruct gender equality. It looks at areas such as politics, work and education, drawing on data from seventy-five countries, covering over 80% of the world's population.

The report revealed that: 'Despite decades of progress in closing the equality gap between men and women, close to *90%* of women, as well as men, hold some sort of bias *against* women.' Around 40–50% of women surveyed stated that they thought that men were better in roles such as political leader or business executive. Wildly, the

---

42   United Nations (2020), 2020 Gender Social Norms Index (GSNI).
    https://hdr.undp.org/content/2020-gender-social-norms-index-gsni

percentages of men with the same belief was roughly the same!

I bet you find these stats hard to believe. They don't make sense, right? I thought that too. I didn't understand it. I dug a bit deeper into the survey, but I didn't find out why this was the case, but then I started to think about it, and the penny dropped.

Women's bias *against* women

We grow up in a world that is biased *towards* men, and therefore inherently biased *against* women. In the main, men and women are unaware of this, and just accept things as they are.

In her fascinating 2020 book *Invisible Women*, Caroline Criado Perez states that 'from government policy and medical research, to technology, workplaces and the media – we are living in a world built *for* and *by* men'.[43] Our world is literally designed for them.

She uses an array of case studies to set out all the ways in which women are overlooked in everyday life in what is essentially a man's world – still. My point here is that we could be almost as unconsciously biased *towards* men (and therefore biased *against* women) in the same way that men are. Both sexes grow up with the same subliminal messages, societal conditioning and programming.

---

43   Caroline Criado Perez (2019), Invisible Women. Chatto & Windus.

Although women are given different messages re our roles in society, we hear many of the same messages about the capabilities of both sexes. But until recently, we also automatically registered that most heads of state, most politicians, most business executives, etc. were men. That gave us the message that men were better for the job – especially top jobs – than women.

However much we consciously believe in women's rights and equality, we've been subconsciously programmed to be biased *towards* men – how screwed up is that? And men, again unconsciously, in having nearly all the power and control for most of the world's history, are automatically biased towards creating systems, processes, organisations, cultures and societies that are suited to their needs, with very little dissent from women – until recently. This is what *both sexes* have absorbed as the norm.

And this has been underlying everything we do. So even if we *consciously think* we're being more gender-aware in raising our children, in the workplace or in the home, there is still some cognitive dissonance due to this unconscious gender bias (unless, of course, you are in the 10% of women who has absolutely no unconscious bias against women).

Imposter syndrome

It occurred to me when I was reading the United Nations report that imposter syndrome, especially around women in business, could be related to this phenomenon.

If most women, as we grew up, were subconsciously taking on board the message that women are fundamentally inferior, weaker or less capable than men, then, no matter how much we *consciously* think of ourselves as capable or have the right qualifications for a particular job, role or career path, our confidence in our abilities is undermined by these subconscious messages about women's innate inadequacy. *We're literally in two minds about ourselves*, having to wrestle with our own long-held negative beliefs about ourselves that undermine our confidence. I've spoken to so many women over the years who have suffered from this, and I've experienced it myself.

I think in practically every job I've ever done, I've felt that I wasn't actually capable of doing it and that I'd be found out – at least, for the first few weeks. This might be something that men also feel, but I found this got worse when it came to becoming a woman in business.

I co-founded an artisan food production business with my husband, and I was very much the front end of the business. I did nearly all of the sales, marketing, PR, trade shows, buyer meetings, etc. I love our products and I found it easy to shout about how wonderful they were, especially when I was at shows talking to members of the public.

But when it came to more official, business-type settings, I felt like a fish out of water, especially if an environment was male-dominated – which they usually were. I felt I had to fake being confident and capable, but I didn't really feel that way inside. The more our business grew, the more often I ended up in these settings. I often felt completely out of my comfort zone, afraid that I would be found out as not being up to the job – of running my own business!

This was highlighted to me when, a few years after we started our business, I was asked to become an ambassador for Women's Enterprise Scotland. I think I laughed when the person asked me. I said something like 'Really? Aren't there businesswomen in Scotland a lot more successful than me, who would be better role models?'

I felt that they might have got me mixed up with someone else, or had the wrong info about me. When it became apparent that it was really me they wanted, my imposter syndrome kicked in big time.

Who was I to be any kind of role model? I was making it up as I went along. What could I teach any women going into business? I was still learning about it all myself. Was I really going to publicly put myself out there as some kind of expert?

My fears were allayed somewhat when I found out that Women's Enterprise Scotland were looking for *real* models, rather than role models: real, relatable women in business who were just starting out themselves or growing businesses, who were often juggling family or other life commitments with business, and who might struggle with confidence, self-belief or self-esteem and were willing to talk to others about it.

I could do that.

They wanted women that other women looking to start (or who'd started) a business, could relate to, rather than people much further down the road (who were already very successful, and women might find it harder to see themselves ever catching up with them).

So I accepted the role, and I'm glad I did. Eight years later, I'm still an ambassador for WES. I've spoken at countless events for them, appeared on television, radio and been in the press. More importantly, though, I've met hundreds of women who've listened to my business story – the ups and downs, the struggles, the wins, the lessons learned – and many have told me that they found my story really helpful. That it helped them believe in themselves more, or that they related to aspects of my story, or that they felt inspired.

Time and time again when I talked to these other women in business, though, imposter syndrome would come up. I would say that the majority of women I know in business have felt it at some point, or continue to feel it, even after they have more than proved themselves. Why is that?

Could it be due to the patriarchal, misogynistic and sexist attitudes we've seen played out in every area of our lives since the day we were born? They might have programmed us to believe that women are inferior, less capable or weaker than men. I think this explains why women usually suffer so much more from imposter syndrome than men, and why it's so hard to think ourselves out of it.

Waking up to our own sexist attitudes

Today, I'm shocked when I think about how much I might have perpetuated what I grew up with. All the roles and structures of my life that have been built on my programming – blindly, until now. Now it makes sense: now I know why I acted as I did. I've passed on much of the subliminal messages and societal conditioning I received unquestioningly to the next generation. In big ways and small, I can see now that all the stereotypes I soaked up in childhood – at home, on television, at school – aren't much different for my children's generation. I feel it's only in the past few years that I've really started to wake up to how little I've done to actively counterbalance those messages.

We're all the products of how we were brought up – including our children. How can we blame young men who are in their teens or twenties now, for the sexism we've been experiencing for decades? They might still be perpetuating it to varying degrees, but is the fact that it was ingrained into them their fault? How can it be their fault if their parents and schools didn't tell them that anything was wrong with these ideas of women, or give them new ideas to replace them?

What if it's partly *our* responsibility because we haven't said anything for all these years. What if, instead of thinking about blame or shame, we all realised that knowing better gives us the chance to do better. The opportunity to make things different going forward. What if it's as much our responsibility to start talking about sexism, to start having the conversations and asking the questions, as it is men's?

What if as well as acknowledging how badly many women have been treated by men, and still are, we also start to explore how can we show the next generation a different way? How can we show boys and men that we don't hate them, and that it's not all their fault, but that they do have to take some responsibility for making things different? How can we help them understand that they can change these ingrained messages and replace them with new attitudes and behaviours, and that things can change for the better?

We need to ask ourselves some hard questions, and be honest with ourselves. We need to see how we've been complicit in keeping attitudes alive simply by tolerating them. There is no shame in this. We're not to blame for our programming, or for being blind to it (that was part of the programming), but when we do see it, we're then responsible for whether or not we keep perpetuating it.

CHAPTER 9

Feminism

Are you a feminist? If you said 'yes' in your head now, would you be as quick to say 'yes' out loud in a mixed-sex group? What about in a group of mostly men? If you'd be more reluctant, or hesitant, why is this? I'm not judging or accusing you in any way if you think you would be more reticent in these situations. Many of us would be – I was for years. It's only in the past few years that I've felt more conviction, ownership and even pride in being a feminist – and that seems strange to me, and also sad, that it took so long.

I can understand why, though. After the 1950s era of the perfect wife/perfect home ideal portrayed in TV programmes and women's magazines, the women's movement of the 1960s heralded what was supposed to be true emancipation for women. With the arrival of freely available contraception, and hippy attitudes towards 'free love' abounding, a lot of women felt free to be more openly sexual. Crucially, at this time there was also an upsurge in activity by women's rights organisations.

When this happened, women's rights came under the spotlight, and there was a backlash. With men, this came in the form of either telling sexist jokes about feminists or by very vocally and aggressively painting them all as angry, men-hating, hairy-legged lesbians that no man would ever want to have sex with. What better way for the patriarchy to dissuade more women from joining the feminist movement than sending the message loud and clear that no man would be interested in her if she declared herself a feminist, or even aligned herself with the cause by showing any support?

Lo and behold, several *anti*-feminist women's organisations sprang up – which men must have loved. Get other women to do the job of fighting the feminists for us – way to go, boys. These other organisations mainly went under the guise of 'protecting family values', and they tried to undermine feminist organisations at every turn. They actively worked against organisations that were just trying to achieve equal rights for women. If that isn't a clear illustration of women's bias against women, I don't know what is.

As you can imagine, though, the women who were actively working against feminist organisations would have been likely to get big brownie points from their husbands and any other men they knew. They would have been lauded for their stance against feminism: *for their stance against equal rights for their own sex*.

Conversely, for women who were supportive of feminist organisations, or even just their principles and ideals, so negative was society's view of these organisations that the women might find themselves on the receiving end of annoyance, disapproval, anger, threats, emotional blackmail or violence from their husbands, and other males in their lives – again, just for publicly agreeing that women should have the same rights as men.

This wasn't a minority, extremist, misogynistic sector of male society that was attacking feminism; this was mainstream, involving men from all walks of life. This view of feminism and feminists was evident in TV programmes (as portrayed in the brilliant 2020 drama series *Mrs America*), in newspapers, in films – and of course, this meant that these views filtered down into living rooms, workplaces, schools and colleges.

What stops a woman calling herself a feminist?

These extreme negative messages about what a feminist is were also programmed into our subconscious from when we were children. Even if we knew that of course feminism was fundamentally a good thing, because it was about equality for women and men (why shouldn't women and men be equal? Surely everyone should want that. And isn't it positive to stand up for women and feminism?). BUT all our conditioning about what a feminist was made it difficult for many women to align themselves with the feminist movement.

I have to own up to the fact that, although I've always felt inside that I'm a feminist (and to be honest, I can't really understand why any woman wouldn't be), I've not done much about that – until now. In my twenties and thirties, I thought of myself as a feminist, but I don't remember ever being very open about it in social settings. Recently, however, I would happily say anywhere that I'm a feminist.

I think my reluctance in the past was threefold. First, I realised that people had a negative view of feminists, and I wasn't sure why it was *so* negative. I didn't really understand then that it was because this view of feminists had been generated by men out of fear of the threat they felt feminism posed (even if they weren't conscious of this). I didn't see that this had been perpetuated for decades, and that most women said nothing about these negative stereotypes of feminists – for the reasons we've just looked at.

I didn't feel confident enough to argue against bad attitudes towards feminism when I was in my twenties and my thirties, so I was never vocal about it. Mostly I didn't have to make a choice about it; I don't remember the subject of feminism ever coming up socially. As I said earlier, though, I tolerated lots of sexist jokes and behaviour over years – socially, in my family and at work – and my reaction was, at most, to show a mild displeasure.

I never really questioned these negative stereotypes of feminists: because I didn't think about it much, but also because I didn't know any women who were ardent feminists. Later in my twenties I made friends with women who were more overtly feminist, and this started to change my impressions through knowledge and understanding – which leads me on to the next reason that I was so reluctant to declare myself a feminist.

Second, I didn't know much about the history of the feminist movement, so I was reluctant to vocalise my alignment to the movement in case someone wanted to engage me in a conversation about things I knew next to nothing about. I had read *Outrageous Acts and Everyday Rebellions* by Gloria Steinem[44] and *Fat is a Feminist Issue* by Susie Orbach[45], but I really felt quite ignorant of what the feminist movement was about. I wish that I'd just kept it simple, as I do now. I think of feminism as believing in equal rights and opportunities for men and women – for all human beings. Full stop. What can be wrong with that? We're all human beings, deserving of the same rights. No group of people should be seen as innately superior merely due to their sex.

Third, and the most embarrassing reason (but I'm going to be honest about it, because I think it's why a lot of young women might not have called themselves feminists): I suspected that if I openly declared myself to be a feminist, then guys would steer clear of me. I would be less likely to be asked out. I wish I hadn't given a rat's ass about that, but my twentysomething self definitely felt this way (and perhaps other women might also have felt

---

44 Gloria Steinem (1985), Outrageous Acts and Everyday Rebellions. Flamingo.
45 Susie Orbach (1988), Fat is a Feminist Issue. Arrow Books.

an element of this). In my teens and twenties, it was all about relationships – friends and boys. So, I wasn't going to do anything that I'd been programmed into thinking would make me less desirable in the eyes of the opposite sex.

But that was then. That was decades ago. I'm talking about being a twentysomething in the late 1980s and 1990s, with the 1970 onwards backlash to feminism still in full swing. I thought that things must be different for young women now. They're more educated about all this stuff, more aware. They've got shouts of 'girl power' ringing in their ears. They're not going to be afraid to proclaim themselves feminists, are they?

Or so I thought.

My son's ex-girlfriend is intelligent, beautiful, friendly and outgoing. She dresses however she pleases, and sometimes that means wearing quite revealing outfits, or all pink, but the reason I mention this is that she is also a feminist, and happy to publicly declare herself one, as are her flatmates (all women in their early twenties).

I had deluded myself that most of the younger generation of girls and women would also now be happy to call themselves feminists. That they would have more understanding of where the bad stereotypes came from and be aware that feminism is basically about equality, and they'd be totally on board with that, since in lots of ways they seem to be more empowered, and better able to vocalise their concerns around inequality, and they now have the platform to do that from.

I had another rude awakening.

The stigma continues

Unfortunately, it seems that my son's ex-girlfriend and her friends are in the minority when it comes to feminist attitudes in the younger generation. According to a range of surveys of various aspects of gender equality, which came out in 2018 and 2019, the number of women aged 18–24 who are happy to call themselves feminists is anywhere from 17% to 57%, depending on the survey you look at.[46] This means that anywhere from 43% to 83% of young women in their late teens or early twenties do not, or would not be happy to, call themselves a feminist.

What? That really took the wind out of my sails. How could that be? Why would young women not want to say they were feminists? Is it for the same reasons that I was reluctant to in my twenties? Are women still programmed with the same negative stereotypes about feminists, or scared to be thought of as man-haters, or worried about the effect that saying they were a feminist might have in relationships with men?

According to many of the women who responded, it is all these reasons.[47] So the patriarchal stereotyping of feminists as hairy, man-hating lesbians is alive and well.

---

46 World Economic Forum (20 June 2023), Global Gender Gap Report 2023. https://www.weforum.org/reports?query=Global+Gender+Gap+Report

47 Dr Christina Scharff (6 February 2019), 'Why so many young women don't call themselves feminist.' https://www.bbc.co.uk/news/uk-politics-47006912

As in any movement, there is a small proportion of feminists with extreme views who fit this stereotype. Some are very vocal about their hatred of men, but they are a minority.

Think of this in relation to religious or political extremists. Just because they exist, that doesn't mean we wouldn't align ourselves with a particular political party or religion, if we believe in its tenets. As a feminist, you are aligning yourself with the belief that women should have the same rights as men, in all spheres of society.

Moving on the messaging

It's only when the messages change to healthy messages about equality for all that the old, ingrained attitudes will changes and girls and women will be happy to say they're feminists, happy to stand up for their rights as women. Also, they need to understand that the negative attitudes they have about feminism are just some more of the sexist messages programmed into us all.

Maybe we need to make sure that everyone knows *why* some people have a negative view of feminism, and what feminism really is: women standing up for the rights of women to be treated equally. That's it. No man-hating, no desire for men to be obliterated from the planet, no need for men to become second-class citizens; just fairness and equality – because women haven't had this for a very, very, very long time.

No arguing about whether there should be equality or not. Just because women have never achieved full equality doesn't mean this is right. Just because the status quo is comfortable doesn't mean it's right. So, budge along the power bench, boys, and make room for us girls. We're here to stay, and we're not going to be ridiculed, mocked, intimidated, threatened, blackmailed or ignored any longer for being feminists. With our heads held high we will happily get on with the work at hand, changing the world for the better day by day. We don't have time for squabbles about power. We don't want to waste our time and energy on defending ourselves; we want to get on with all that we're brilliant at. Watch us go!

You don't have to have *I'm a Feminist* printed on a T-shirt. You don't have to announce it everywhere you go. Instead, start having conversations about what you've read here with other women. Start talking to younger people about it. Allow yourself to wake up to the difference that *you* can make by this simple shift in how you think of yourself.

Going into the history of feminism and talking about the incredible women who worked tirelessly so that women can have the freedoms and rights we enjoy today, or looking at all the feminist ideologies is outwith the scope of this book. There are some brilliant books and online resources, though, if you'd like to learn more about this movement that we all owe so much to.

One more thing you can do is to keep up to date with women's rights and concerns by signing up to the newsletters of the organisations that are fighting on our behalf. A quick google of feminist organisations will throw up an array that are working for equality in a variety of ways. Some focus on raising awareness of sexism and gender stereotyping in schools, some on media representation, some on making the justice system fairer, and others work on a range of issues – so whatever bothers you most of the array of battles that women are fighting, there will be an organisation addressing this that you can support.

Most of these organisations will have information and resources that will enable you to get involved in creating the change you want to see in your community – and in the world.

CHAPTER 10

Where do we go from here?

Throughout this book, I've explored some of the commonalities in our experiences of being a woman at this time in the Western world. I wanted to put into words all that has been swimming around in my head over decades, concerns and questions about why things are the way they are for women. I wanted to try to answer some of the questions that seem difficult to answer. I wanted to say what seems to go unsaid. I wanted to try to understand better, to try to make sense of it all. I wanted to feel less confused about it. I still don't have many answers, but I do have a greater understanding, ideas, and a growing sense of the possibilities for change. Hopefully you do too. I hope you feel that you have a lot more than you might have thought in common with other women: we are all struggling with similar issues and having similar experiences.

We've looked at the pervasive poison of sexism and the patriarchy and how, collectively, we've got to where we are through our unconscious programming. We've looked at how we might have perpetuated some patriarchal messages, and sexism, and why things are getting worse, rather than better, in many ways, for the younger generation. Alongside this, we explored the inequality and injustice that still exist for women at work and at home.

If we have woken up to all this and do nothing about it, then not much is likely to change, particularly in our own lives. Of course, we can leave it up to the organisations that are already working in the field and hope they make the differences we hope to see, but is that enough? Can we do something about all this, either individually or collectively? What could we do differently in our own lives to create change for ourselves and others? What if we could each be a small part of the solution – collectively, we could make a big difference. What if we could make a difference not just in the lives of the girls and boys who are heading towards adulthood currently, but also in our own lives?

In this book we have been on a journey, but I hope you can see that, rather than it coming to an end, this is only the beginning. What do we need to move forward?

The antidote

It seems to me that to move forward we need a three-pronged approach, and I'll discuss each in the next three chapters. These will be the antidote to the poison that is our sexist, patriarchal culture.

The first prong is waking up to the cognitive dissonance we have been experiencing, thanks to our patriarchal conditioning, and beginning to recognise how this conditioning has played out in our lives and how we might unwittingly have perpetuated it. In doing this, we reduce our cognitive dissonance – and can begin to change our perceptions and beliefs.

The second is finally recognising our own worth as women, as human beings, distinct from the way we've been taught to value ourselves by society: realising that having a true, solid, reliable sense of our own worth is nothing to do with how we look, or how close we are to being the 'ideal woman' or conforming to any roles that have been imposed on us.

The third prong is coming into our own personal power: building our mental and emotional strength, and our sense of our own abilities, then using that power to create change in our own lives – or wider society. Even if this just means beginning to have conversations with family and friends, perhaps making others more aware of our programming and the cognitive dissonance at play. Even if it just means deciding to tolerate less and speak up more on a daily basis.

It all makes a difference.

Let's dive in.

CHAPTER 11

Wake up! Cognitive dissonance

I've mentioned cognitive dissonance quite a few times. That's because it feels so important. I feel that understanding this is key to waking up to our conditioning. To recap, it's feeling a mental tension, a sense of anxiety or stress, or physically uncomfortable because of new information, perceptions, attitudes or behaviours that conflict with your established beliefs and long-held ingrained attitudes.

When it comes to sexism and the patriarchy, in Chapter 7 we looked at how we've been programmed to subconsciously believe that men *are* actually superior to women, and therefore that we are somehow less than them as a sex: less important, intelligent, capable, etc.

If this has been ingrained into us since the day we were born, then when we become aware of sexism, or encounter it, even when in our gut we know it's wrong, our conscious thoughts about it clash with our subconscious beliefs. If we want to speak up or act on something we feel is unjust, we might feel anxious, uncomfortable or full of fear that we are doing something wrong – because this new information is creating a cognitive dissonance. We're confronting our mind with the new information that we shouldn't be treated this way, that we are equal, that the behaviour or language we have witnessed is sexist and inappropriate, but thinking there is something *wrong* with this has been the opposite of our conditioning.

So we're less likely to challenge any sexism we see or experience, or speak up openly about inequality, or actively call ourselves feminists because subconsciously this feels like we would be going against our own deep perceptions and beliefs. So how do we change this?

Let's compare it to smoking. Years ago, before we all knew better, smoking was seen as cool. People grew up seeing some of the greatest actors on TV smoking and looking cool. The messages they had absorbed about smoking were that it was a grown-up thing to do, that it was sophisticated, that it was soothing and calming.

All this, of course, was clever marketing of exactly these ideals and rewards by the tobacco industry, to get people hooked to an addictive substance and create a habit that might be lifelong, generating huge revenues for the industry.

Initially, when messages about how bad smoking actually was for you began to surface, smokers denied them. They called it scaremongering, and there was no way they were going to give up their precious addiction (which, until now, they probably hadn't seen as an addiction.) However, when smokers began to see that the tobacco industry had actively fed them their beliefs about smoking for years and years, they could start to change their attitudes and beliefs about smoking. It would take a while for the masses of studies and articles about the dangers of smoking, and the brainwashing regarding it, to filter deeper into people's consciousness and make them change their beliefs and wake them up to what was actually going on. The more they did, the more likely it was that someone would give up smoking. There would be less cognitive dissonance in them. They had woken up to the reality that cigarettes and smoking were bad for them.

Likewise, with the ingrained sexist and patriarchal ideas and attitudes we've absorbed since childhood, when we wake up to what has been going on and how blind we've been to it, then we reduce the cognitive dissonance in our own minds. An awareness of this programming, seeing it for what it is and seeing how it could create cognitive dissonance in us is enough to begin to dismantle some of the programming and reduce the dissonance.

We can start to unravel the unhealthy – and plain wrong – unconscious beliefs and attitudes we've had about ourselves as women. We can start to see what has really happened and why we've been reluctant to use our voices, to stand up for equality and fully inhabit our place in the world as equals.

We're less likely to feel uncomfortable about standing up for ourselves and other women when we wake up to the insidiousness of all we have absorbed over the years – and can see it for what it is. The less cognitive dissonance there is, the less discomfort we feel. We're making ourselves aware that there has been an internal conflict within us.

That we've been going against ourselves – or at least, not standing up for ourselves in ways we could have – because we've been programmed not to.

Awareness is the first step to reducing cognitive dissonance. Awareness is the floodlight that shows you the reality that was previously in the shadows. But we knew there was something wrong. Our instincts told us that many of our experiences of what it means to be a woman in our world today just weren't right. Becoming aware of what has really been going on just confirms it for us.

The penny drops, the lightbulb goes on, and we realise it wasn't something wrong with us, or that we were alone, or that we were going crazy because others weren't talking about things being wrong or that men couldn't seem to see how unacceptable a lot of their behaviours were. We realise that we've been asleep to how sexism and the patriarchy has been playing out in our lives, but now we've woken up.

All of the above obviously also equally applies to men, as I talked about in Chapter 7. They are even less likely to have seen sexism and patriarchal conditioning for what they are – and they are likely to experience cognitive dissonance to an even greater degree when they are faced with attitudes that contradict their programming. But by being aware of this programming, and aware of the cognitive dissonance, there is no reason they can't begin to understand why things are the way they are – and why things need to be different, for the benefit of us all.

Even for men who aren't guilty of particularly sexist behaviours or who actively support women's rights, being aware of their programming and cognitive dissonance might make them more likely to challenge sexist behaviours in other men, or talk about it to others, or to be more vocal in support of women. It's worth a shot.

CHAPTER 12

Knowing your worth

The second thing we can do is to counterbalance our objectification – our conditioning as an object to be admired, judged or criticised for how we look. The answer lies in developing a true sense of our own worth. One of the most successful marketing campaigns of all time is L'Oréal's 'Because you're worth it!' campaign. This is one of the few marketing slogans that has stood the test of time; we still hear it more than fifty years after it was first used (originally 'because I'm worth it').

Ironically, the tagline is purported to be about self-empowerment, about women doing things for themselves to benefit their self-esteem rather than to please the male gaze; but it's used to sell products such as hair dye and face creams, perpetuating the messages we've been fed that our worth lies in the way we look – and the younger and prettier you look, the more you're worth.

Your true worth does not lie in the labels and roles you have acquired throughout your life. Neither does it lie in the way you look, or how young you look. Your worth as a human being and as a woman does not lie in the colour or style of your hair, the size of your thighs / belly / breasts / upper arms / waist, the straightness or whiteness of your teeth, the size of your lips, your lack of body hair, how tall/short/fat/thin you are, the type of clothes you wear or how you look in them, whether you wear make-up or not, whether you exercise or not, or in how quiet / loud / 'ladylike' or 'unladylike' you are.

As you go about your day – as you get dressed, look at yourself in the mirror, or apply make-up, or any time when you are conscious of how you look, or have negative feelings about how you look, or how you might appear – *remind yourself of the above.*

Remember that you are assessing and judging yourself through the lens of the societal conditioning that has dictated to you since birth *that the ideal woman should look a certain way, and you should constantly measure yourself against that standard.* Then remind yourself that now you can see that, you don't need to be a slave to it any more. You've freed yourself. Remind yourself that your worth isn't tied up in any of this, and that you're much more than all of this. Remind yourself of all the things that your worth lies in.

Your worth lies in your basic humanity: in being a human being living on this planet, at this time, struggling with what you struggle with, juggling all that you juggle, dealing with all that you deal with – and getting up each day and doing it all again.

Your worth lies in being able to extend yourself to connect with, or be of service to, others when you need to, or feel able to, but also in appreciating and taking care of your precious self. Your worth lies in all that you create in the world – whether that's creating artistically, in the work you do, or in the home. You create the world and the life around you day by day. If you are unhappy with any aspects of your life, broaden your focus and think about all that you have created in your life to date, and all the experiences you've gone through.

Your worth lies in how you've developed and grown as a person and the lessons you have learned from life, sometimes in really hard ways. It lies in your willingness to keep growing and learning. Your worth lies in your capacity to love and to give: not out of a sense of duty, or at the cost of your own well-being, but from knowing your own heart, and cultivating self-love, as well as giving love to others.

All of these are the antidote to the poison of seeing yourself through the eyes of the patriarchal society that you've grown up in. To help you stop following the programming that's told you to value yourself first and foremost for the way you look. The way in which we value ourselves can be so ingrained in us, though, that at first it's hard to imagine *not* looking at ourselves through that lens. But it's exactly what we need to do if we want to step away from objectifying ourselves.

Obviously, this doesn't mean you need to stop caring about how you look. It doesn't mean that you can't wear make-up, dye your hair, pay attention to the clothes you wear, get a fake tan, or whatever you want to do. But getting a different perspective on these things – seeing how we've been indoctrinated into seeing these things as tied to our worth – means we see them for what they are. Our self-esteem, our sense of our worth as a human being, is not tied to these things. The stranglehold that this can have on us eases, and with it comes more of a sense of ease.

If you don't feel that you *have to* do everything that constitutes your beauty, diet, body and clothing routines, you can relax and realise that it's your choice. Whether you do them or not will not alter your worth one iota.

Building true self-esteem

Often, if we buy a new outfit, are acknowledged for a project we've worked hard on, do something to help someone else, or lose a bit of weight, we feel a boost in our self-esteem. We feel better about ourselves, we feel more confident – like we're 'winning at life'. This usually only lasts for a short time, though. As you know, all too soon, you have a bad hair day, you hear an unkind remark, you have a setback at work, and you just don't feel as good; you begin to feel bad about yourself instead. Your confidence has taken a knock and you feel that you're now somehow failing at life.

This isn't true self-esteem if it can fluctuate so wildly and so easily. *This is ego.* This swinging between thinking we're great – or at least okay – in an area of our lives to thinking we're awful is all in our head. The clue is in *thinking.* Whether we think well or badly of ourselves, our self-concept – how we *think* of ourselves, and how we *think* we're thought of by others – is an idea in our head.

Often, this idea has been formed from our assessment of how well we measure up to society's idea of how we're supposed to be, and look.

We live on automatic pilot, constantly judging and assessing how well we are measuring up to society's ideals of womanhood. Not just in how we look or behave, but in our roles: how we are as employees, or mothers, or daughters, or colleagues. We keep absorbing the messages that continue, and cement, all the subliminal messages we've absorbed since childhood.

Ego is most often thought of in terms of someone 'having a big ego', but we all have an ego. It's our mental concept of ourself. So yes, if we feel we look good, it's a boost to our ego. And if we feel we look awful, our ego is deflated. We can't get rid of our ego, but if we see what it really is – a collection of thoughts about ourselves, skewed by fluctuating perceptions from outside ourselves – we realise that's not who we really are. Which is why our self-esteem should not be anchored to our ego.

The things I talked about above regarding where your sense of your true worth lies – that's where your self-esteem needs to be anchored. The more you build up your sense of worth as relating to all the internal aspects of who you are as a human being and as a woman, the stronger your self-esteem will be. You will have confidence in your worth and abilities, and you will feel more able to express that. It will be true self-esteem. It will be constant and will build over time, rather than inflate and deflate depending on external circumstances.

Then you can enjoy feeling good about yourself more consistently, based on real, true aspects of yourself or how you live your life. You will have a richer, deeper feeling of your value as a person. That's true self-esteem.

On occasions when you also feel good about how you look, for whatever reason, that can be a good feeling and an added bonus, but you don't *need* it to feel good about yourself, because you already do. You can enjoy it, but you know that it doesn't mean anything about who you are as a person.

CHAPTER 13

Personal power

You might be fifty or fifteen, and you might think of yourself as a feminist – or you might not. However, whether or not you believe that women are still struggling with the challenges of sexism and inequality in society (if you don't, seriously, have you read the rest of this book?), you must at least see that *some* of the hope for change around the sexism, patriarchal structures, attitudes and behaviours that we experience lies with women.

It's not that it's our *responsibility*; it's that we have the *opportunity* to make a difference – for ourselves, for how we experience our lives, for other women, and for the girls and young women who follow us. Of course, men bear the most responsibility to understand what's happening, change their attitudes and behaviours, and affect change in other men and wider society, but women can add to what they do, and we can be catalysts for men to reach a better understanding or to instigate change. We can accelerate the process of change with our voice and actions. We can also be directors of further change.

But how can women best contribute to any change? The answer lies in our power as individuals. The more you can sense your own personal power, as a human being and as a woman, the more able you'll feel to create change in your world. Imagine if you and I, and our female relatives, friends, work colleagues and acquaintances all came into their own personal power. What could we do together?

I'm not talking about manipulative or coercive power. I'm not talking about flipping the tables and women becoming more like men. (That would change the dynamic but would not solve the problems.)

Personal power is *not* about being aggressive, violent, bullying, controlling, superior, authoritarian or dominant. It *is* about being compelling, energetic, influential, persuasive, capable, strong, dynamic, effective, forceful and commanding.

What I'm talking about is your own authentic power as a human being. The power to claim your right to dignity, respect, fair treatment, and equality with other human beings, and to recognise your inherent worth as a magnificent, complex, capable, woman.

Our own personal power is multi-faceted. We can come to recognise and appreciate it by various routes, and strengthen and deepen our experiences of it in different ways. Everyone can access their own personal power, and the more you recognise, accept and cultivate it, the stronger it becomes – you literally grow it, like a plant. Developing your personal power will lead you to who you truly are, and to your inherent inner worth, and you won't have to chase any external sources of validation.

Your personal power isn't an idea, a feeling, a thought or a concept; it is the core of you. It's the energy of your authentic self, who you really are under all the labels that society gives you (which are more about your roles and the outer shell that the world sees, rather than who you really are inside).

Your labels begin with 'daughter', 'granddaughter' and maybe 'sister' or 'niece'. Then move on to possibly 'mother', 'aunt' or 'gran'. Then you are given, or you choose, labels based on how you behave in the world, so these might be 'quiet', 'shy', 'friendly', 'volatile', 'adventurous', 'timid', etc. Later your labels might be related to the work you do, or your hobbies. All these layers of labels – some of which you might like, some which you might hate – become your identity. They say something about you so that the world can get a handle on who you are – but they are not who you *actually* are.

These labels are in your head, and other people's heads, and they only mean something if you want them to. You can choose to let go of the labels and have a more authentic experience of life by developing a better relationship to your own body, and your own self, rather than the concepts that other people have of you.

But I digress. If you're interested in learning more about this, I have written a book on this topic.[48]

---

48 Lynn B. Mann (2021), BEING: Awake, aware, and experiencing life as your authentic self. Being Books.

For the purposes of this book, though, you just need to look at all the labels you have, and the roles you carry out in your life. Write two lists: one with your labels and one with your roles. Write as many as you can think of in one sitting, then you can add to them over the coming days as you think of more.

As you look at the lists, let it sink in that these labels aren't who you *really* are; they're only what the world sees you as. And maybe also what you think the world expects you to be. You need to realise that you're also something else, over and above all these things, and underneath all these things. This is where your personal power lies.

The more you can remind yourself of who you really are, and sense your innate power – who you are beyond the labels and roles – the more you will strengthen that personal power. This can make you feel stronger and more capable, even before you do anything with this power. You feel its potential spark inside you, and you realise that there is more to you than you'd previously thought.

My two selves

By way of illustration, the following is how I see my personal power, my authentic self, now that I have finally emerged from the societally programmed, conditioned self that I'd tried to squeeze myself into being for the first several decades of my life. It started with my parents, as my two most influential role models as I grew up.

My view of my parents was as follows:

1. My mum: a paragon of virtue – very loving, kind,
    reserved, modest, generous, friendly, patient and
    good-natured. A care-giver through and through.
    She was mostly a full-time mum, but she also ran
    a baby clothes shop for a few years when I was
    in my teens, and later for several years ran my
    parents' hotel. Teetotal. Everyone loved her.

2. My dad: not so much a paragon of virtue – often
    loud, verbose, selfish and opinionated, very
    much 'a man's man', he mostly hung out with
    large groups of men at the pub, or latterly in our
    own hotel. A heavy drinker. Also very soft-
    hearted, generous and a bit eccentric (he did
    things like rescuing a great Dane one day when
    he was stopped at traffic lights because he was
    talking to the owner, who said they couldn't
    afford to feed the dog anymore, so he arrived
    home with it!). I think I can safely say that he was
    an original, and a character, but he certainly
    wasn't everyone's cup of tea.

Mum and Dad seemed like polar opposites. They
didn't have many interests in common, yet they loved each
other very much and they were very good parents. These
profiles of them illustrate where I see the struggle was
born in me between the idea of the me I thought I *should*
be – as a girl, as a woman – and my more real, true self.
I'm not sure when I first became aware of the forces at

odds within me – probably some time in my teens. I could feel a pull between what I was supposed to, or was expected to do, and what I really wanted to do. It wasn't simply a teenage rebellion, pushing against the rules and restrictions of family as I felt a growing need for independence – although there was that too. This was more about my identity, and about being female.

I think it was to do with the fact that I thought I was 'supposed to' be more like my mum because I was female, and because she embodied the patriarchal stereotype of the ideal woman, wife and mother. I was supposed to emulate her simply because I was a girl, regardless of my character and personality. I was supposed to behave like her, be 'ladylike', quiet, gentle, not be 'too much' and not be too exuberant or outspoken.

I often felt that I was just too much. This wasn't expressed to me in very obvious ways; it was more in little comments, looks and passing remarks. Not just from my immediate family but also from my wider family, at school and at clubs. I don't remember thinking about this very much, just feeling a sense of annoyance, of disapproval from others – a sense that, somehow, I was wrong to be the person I felt I really was.

My natural personality often seemed more of a male way to be. If you were a boy, you could be loud and exuberant and too much – yet you could also be yourself. Ah, sorry, I didn't get that memo. But I got away with it when I was younger, when I was a tomboy – I hung around with boys, climbed trees, rode bikes, collected tadpoles, pinched fruit from people's gardens, and basically had lots of adventures. And as I mentioned earlier, since I had short hair and I was tall for my age, I was regularly mistaken for a boy.

As I grew older, my parents – being the loving parents they were, and thinking they were bringing me up properly – kept slipping the memo under my nose. I would metaphorically nod and feel guilty for being too much, and I would simmer down, change my behaviour, be quieter – whatever was required – until the next time, and the next time...

I felt much more like my dad, though. Without vocalising it or understanding it, I felt more aligned to the life that he lived: a life of projects, being here, there and everywhere, meeting lots of people from all walks of life. He always had lots of ideas that he was exploring or pursuing, but I didn't understand how that was supposed to translate into my life. Also, crucially, I think I could see that *he just got to be himself*: he more or less did whatever he wanted to, whenever he wanted to.

This set up in me a very unhealthy battle between trying to be the girl I felt I was expected to be – and being myself. Mostly, I suppressed the wilder, freer, more dynamic aspects of my personality. Throughout my teens, I kept in line. I behaved like a societally conditioned female teenager: be polite and friendly to everyone; do well academically; don't get into trouble; have 'nice' friends that your parents approve of; be sporty or have hobbies; go to Brownies, Guides or church; don't drink alcohol or take drugs; don't have sex before you're married. Oh, and while doing all this, most of all, don't wear any weird clothes or put on weight.

So, I toed the line (mostly). I think my friends from then would say I still managed to be pretty loud and bossy, and full on when I wanted to be – well, I suppose I was when I was around them, but I felt that I was largely being a 'good girl'. It wasn't until I left school and started working and studying that I really found my freedom, but this new me was a problem. I didn't know what to do with the wilder, freer, more adventurous part of me that began to emerge. I was scared of her. I didn't trust myself. I think I felt like she would overwhelm me if I gave her free rein. I had to control her. Enter bulimia, stage left (as I mentioned earlier). All the while I partied hard, had various jobs, 'found' alcohol, travelled around the world, then finally met my now husband when I was twenty-nine.

I'm telling you this summary of my story because the chaos of my late teens and twenties need not have been such a self-destructive, damaging time for me. I can see that it was my entrenched societal conditioning that created the struggle in me, that created the 'good girl/bad girl' feelings in me. Later, I realised that this struggle was more about who I thought I was supposed to be versus who I felt I really was.

All the gender pigeonholes that we are squeezed into by society (and our families and school) make us repress the more vibrant, real, authentic parts of our own character and personality – and *these* are our personal power. The loss of these or the inability to express these festers inside us, causing psychological and emotional damage.

I feel sad for younger me, who was often so full of self-loathing. Having burst free of some of the boundaries of my conditioning, so I was more able to be my true self, I didn't know what to do with the self that I had suppressed for so long. I didn't know how to just *be* myself. I was terrified of the strength, the power, the passion of that true self, and I didn't know what to do with her.

I thought that these aspects of myself were somehow bad or wrong because they didn't fit in with society's version of how a girl or a woman should be. I did what most women do when they feel confusion or pain at not being able to be themselves: I blamed myself and turned these feelings in on myself. I focused on changing how I behaved, and how I looked, to try to be a different version of me, to try to be the woman I had been programmed to be.

Getting to know yourself

Part of accessing your personal power is figuring out what you really, really want, what you like, what your purpose and passions might be, and how you want to express these in your life. You have to explore what motivates and inspires you personally. These are the jigsaw puzzle pieces you need to create a full picture of your true self, where your personal power lies, rather than your societally prescribed self.

As an example of this, as I told you at the beginning, I didn't intend writing this book. I didn't want to write this book. It seemed like too huge a task, so I told myself I *shouldn't* try to write this book. I tried to convince myself that it would be safer and easier and more sensible to stick to my plan of writing what I'd intended to write. That was my head talking. In my heart, though, I couldn't let go of the idea of this book. I felt compelled to write it. I felt that I couldn't *not* write it.

Getting more in touch with my authentic self over the past few years meant that I paid attention to that impulse, to that compulsion, and changed the book I was writing. I know that I've a multitude of thoughts and strong feelings and many, many experiences related to the subject matter. I have lots to say and I want to say it – regardless of how it will be received. My job, my purpose and my passion is to say what I feel I need to say about it, and put it out there – then it's out of my hands and I've done my part by following the voice of my authentic self, using my personal power to express what I wanted to express, and being true to myself. How the book is then received in the world – whether people love it, hate it, or anywhere in between – is out of my hands.

It took me a while to trust my instincts, to do what feels like the right thing at any given time. It was a process of realising that I was more than all the labels and roles I had, then beginning to find my true self in my true desires. The next step is owning it. And the same is true for you.

Taking yourself seriously

In our family, and I know many others, a common phrase we heard growing up was 'children should be seen and not heard'. Apparently this phrase originated in the fifteenth century, where only young women (surprise, surprise!) were supposed to stay silent in the presence of adults and speak only when they were spoken to, but it later evolved to include all children.

I find it incredible to think that it was still being used only a few decades ago. I wonder if it is still used today. What does it say to children? 'Your thoughts don't matter. We don't care about your opinions. You have nothing to say that we want to hear.'

Don't get me wrong. Having raised two children and been around lots more, there are many, many times when I wished I could have switched them off! The noise level, the intense chatter, the stage when they ask a constant stream of questions...

It wasn't just the 'children should be seen and not heard' phrase that served to squash children's self-expression. There are myriad ways in which children are discouraged from having a voice or thinking that their opinions matter. Children, especially girls, are often given the message that what they think and feel, and their ideas, hopes and dreams, or their ambition, are not taken seriously.

Over the past couple of decades, things do seem to have started to improve for girls and young women, even though there is still some way to go. Before then, young women had limits put on them in terms of further education, career paths, job opportunities and the business world. Previously the most common careers for women were as secretaries, nurses, waitresses or teachers. Very few were police officers, accountants, lawyers or doctors.[49]

Yes, many women pushed against that and got into universities, organisations or fields of study that were traditionally male-dominated. Often they were the sole woman. However, it has been well publicised that their experiences were sometimes awful, because of the appalling ways they were often treated by men: rather than encouraging other women to follow them, they were dissuaded.

Even though I messed about a lot at school, and was more interested in my friends, music and boys than my schoolwork, I passed all my exams with mostly As. I vaguely remember the careers guidance person telling me that I might want to think about going to university, but I didn't have a clue what that entailed, why I would want to, or what job I'd want to do afterwards. I didn't know a single person who had gone to university, and neither did any of my family. My dad said he didn't see the point in my going to university unless I wanted to be a lawyer, a doctor or something similar, so why didn't I just get a job? So, I did.

It's a whole other world now with regard to university. Many young people go, not knowing what they want to do

---

49 Mehroz Baig (2013), 'Women in the workforce: What changes have we made?' Huffpost, https://www.huffpost.com/entry/women-in-the-workforce-wh_b_4462455

afterwards, but many plan their run-up to university like a military operation. They take it very seriously. But that's a good thing. I don't think I took myself seriously enough, in terms of what I was capable of, what I could do with my life and what I could create in it, until I was well into my thirties – which is when I went to uni.

I didn't realise I hadn't been taking myself seriously, until I began to. I had been working part-time as a therapist, then the agency I worked for closed down. Our son was ten and our daughter was two, so I decided to take a career break, but around the same time my husband Chris was looking at ideas for starting an on-farm diversification.

We live on a small, tenanted farm. This means we don't own it, but the farm has been in his family for 175 years and it has been passed down through five generations. Chris was looking to add another income stream, so he explored various possibilities, one of which was producing cold pressed rapeseed oil on the farm.

To cut a long story short, I decided to help him with it for a year until our daughter was at nursery, just to get it off the ground. I said I'd help him to get our oil into a few local shops and have a stall at a few farmers' markets. However, I ended up going to networking events, then joined a food and drink trade body, and started to meet buyers. All the while I thought of myself as a farmer's wife who just happened to be a people person, and I was getting lucky with customers because we had a great product. I didn't credit myself with any success we were having. I had no strategy, intelligence, application or flair, as far as I was concerned; I was just lucky.

It was only when a friend encouraged me to join a business accelerator programme for start-up businesses that I learned about the mindsets and behaviours of entrepreneurs. Then one of the programme mentors challenged me when I attributed our growing business successes to 'luck', and I started to own some responsibility for that success.

It was as if, through the lens of their descriptions of desirable qualities in entrepreneurs and business people, I could start to recognise those traits in myself and see how my experience in my twenty-two jobs had given me valuable skills and developed me as a person. And that I'd drawn on those skills in helping to set up, and grow, our food business. I began to appreciate that it was more than just luck that had led us to develop the business into a much bigger concern than we thought it would be. At first, we envisaged it as a sideline that might bring in a little extra income.

And this process opened the floodgates in me. If I hadn't gone through this process of realising my own strengths, I don't think I'd have done any of what came next. I'd never have had the self-belief, the confidence, the sense of my own ability, of my own innate personal power.

What happened over the next eight years was that the business became a successful, multi-award-winning food business that now supplies hotels, restaurants and shops throughout the UK and further afield, and that retails online. As well as working in Supernature Oils, I also developed a social enterprise called Food For Good which was designed to bring the food industry together to help address food poverty. I passed it on to another social enterprise before I launched it, as it was growing arms and legs, and my newfound sense of my own capabilities was drawing me more and more towards a writing project that I'd started ten years earlier, when I worked as a therapist. I let go of Food For Good so I could finish my first book, *BEING: Awake, aware, and experiencing life as your authentic self.*

I don't think I would have committed myself to writing that book if I hadn't co-founded Supernature and founded Food For Good. Somehow, I had to have those experiences to be able to believe in myself, take myself seriously, and come into my own personal power. Maybe this was because, as a woman, I already thought I was less capable. Maybe it was because I had flitted from job to job throughout my twenties; I thought I wasn't any good at anything or there wasn't 'the right thing for me' out there. I don't know.

What I do know is that today I know what I'm capable of, I'm creating what I want in my life, and I'm absolutely loving it. Even though I'm in my fifties, it feels like I'm just getting started with all that I want to do – and can do. There's no stopping me.

Although I've been talking about taking myself seriously, and I want you to take yourselves seriously, I hope you realise I definitely don't mean this in a heavy or arrogant way. Certainly not in a superior way. It's much more about knowing your own worth, valuing yourself and appreciating all that you are capable of. It's about inhabiting, then unleashing, your authentic self. It's a good feeling. A feeling of knowing that you can create what you want to create in life.

If you realise that you've not been taking yourself seriously, whether you think this is because of how you were brought up, your schooling, your societal conditioning, other people's influence on you, or something else, the good thing is that you recognise it now. You can start to take yourself more seriously by building up a picture of all your capabilities, and you can begin to see that you're more powerful than you have given yourself credit for.

Finding your voice

I think finding your voice is about expressing your personal power. Your voice isn't just what you say. Your voice is how you express yourself in everything you do. It can be in what you create, or in your actions and reactions. It's about knowing what motivates you to speak up or express yourself – perhaps in anger, with passion, maybe in frustration, excitedly, or with hope, or with a vision for how things could be different … in one small thing or in some huge way.

Your voice is about what you choose to align yourself with, to become part of, to support, fundraise for or campaign for. You might use your voice simply to change things for yourself, how you feel about yourself or how you live your life. You might use it to effect change in your immediate or wider family, or your local community, or in your city, or in the world.

Usually, we find our voice by cultivating our relationship to our authentic self, but sometimes it works the other way. You might feel drawn to change your life in a particular way, or to create something, or to work with a group or organisation. You might not know why this particular project or cause feels right for you, but it helps you move towards being your authentic self. You may instinctively feel that you've found something you connect with and that you can channel your real self into. This again can help you to find your voice and become more attuned to it.

I say 'attuned to it' because your voice isn't a voice you hear in your head, that speaks to you – although it can be. It's like a frequency that you tune into. Your voice can come to you in a hunch, or a desire, or in feeling compelled to do something that feels right for you – even though on paper, in your head or to others it doesn't make much sense. It's where you tune into your truest self then express that in the world, in whichever form you choose.

Your voice is your instinct for what is right *for you*, your intuition for what matters *to you*, regardless of how it's seen by others. It can develop from a feeling in your gut, or a queasiness in your stomach, or seeing red and deciding that enough is enough, or in a million other ways.

Whatever the catalyst is, if you stay with the promptings of your authentic self, at some point you will use your voice to do something about whatever has caused this emotional reaction in you.

When it comes to using your authentic voice proactively in the world, you might choose to focus on what *you* see as an injustice, about an indignity or humiliation *you* have felt that you want to prevent others from feeling, or from pain and suffering you see around you, or in the wider world, that you want to do something about.

You don't have to commit to doing a grand act. You might even decide to do something about one of your relationships, or within your family, rather than out in the world. What matters is having that impetus, that burning desire for things to be different.

Of course, there's an alternative. We always have the option to anaesthetise our internal voices, the promptings of our true selves, with some carbs or some booze, or by binge-watching some TV, or by distracting ourselves online, or by going shopping, or … whatever. We've all been there, bought the T-shirt.

But when the moment passes, you won't feel the same urge to do anything. You won't need to put your head above the parapet. You'll also miss out on all that comes with fulfilling your potential by living life as your authentic self, and owning your personal power.

Being a FREE woman

As long as you're not incarcerated and don't live in a country where there is no freedom of speech, you have the opportunity to be a free woman.

What does being a free woman mean? There are two aspects to it. The first is waking up to the illusions that we've been programmed with, that we've bought into, since the day we were born. That includes waking up to our part in perpetuating sexism and patriarchal ideals and attitudes.

When you wake up and see what you've been shackled to for most of your life, the shackles don't have such a hold on you anymore. You've taken the first step in dismantling your cage of societal conditioning.

The second aspect of being a free woman lies in knowing your true worth and coming into your personal power. It lies in understanding, recognising, owning and acting as your real, true self. In looking honestly at what brings joy, happiness, satisfaction or fulfilment into your life – and what doesn't.

It's only by doing this that we become free to be ourselves, which I think is the ultimate freedom. To be free to fully inhabit your body, to love and accept that body, to know that your worth doesn't lie in how you look, to know your true worth, to find your voice, and to express yourself openly and honestly. To make choices based on what feels right for you, not what you think you 'should' be doing.

Coming into your own, waking up to where you are and where you've come from, appreciating yourself for all that you are and owning your authentic power sets you free. Free from the chains of your patriarchal conditioning. As a free woman, you feel comfortable in your own skin. You have respect for yourself, so you are less likely to tolerate others disrespecting you. You know that first and foremost you are a human being who deserves to be appreciated and celebrated.

CHAPTER 14

The core of equality

What I've been building a picture of in the past few chapters is female empowerment. Waking up. Knowing our worth. Owning our personal power. Being free.

Female empowerment is the core of equality. Each and every one of us has the right to equality. To be treated the same as others, as a human being.

That's why being a feminist isn't about man-hating, or man-bashing, or only about focusing on wrongs to women, and expecting men to deal with sexism and our patriarchal culture. Of course, we don't discount men's culpability for the misogyny, sexism and violence they've perpetrated. Of course, each one needs to wake up to their own – and other men's – sexist attitudes and behaviours, and take responsibility for doing something about them.

However, if we take all that as a given and say 'this is how bad it's been, and this is how bad it still is in some ways'. If we acknowledge the terror, abuse and violence that many, many women have suffered at the hands of men, and are still suffering. If we acknowledge the patriarchal systems and organisations that are the framework of our lives have been biased against women, and that things need to change, structurally and systemically, in our society. And if we acknowledge the multitude of ways in which women have been treated unfairly because of our sexist, patriarchal society, then, while we are trying to right these wrongs, while we support the people and organisations fighting for justice, or to extend or protect women's rights, to change laws, to overhaul legal and justice systems, we can also consider how we can make things different in our own lives right now – and for the future. We become proactive: we take responsibility for changing our own thinking, our attitudes, our behaviours, and for influencing the people in our lives.

Let's face it: things are likely to change a lot faster when empowered women focus on ways to create different experiences and galvanise other women rather than passively waiting for things to change.

We need to wake up to all the horseshit we've been fed about who we're supposed to be, and how we're supposed to behave, and how we're supposed to look. Here's an idea: how about we stop buying into it and start accepting and loving ourselves for who we are, regardless of how we look? How about we do the same for other women, and realise that they are the same as us, fighting the same bullshit? How about we urge our daughters, nieces, friends and relatives not to buy into it anymore?

The beginning of the end for this illusion we've been force-fed is awareness – *seeing* it. If you see it, help others to see it. It's only by seeing it that you can begin to let go of it, and get a different perspective on yourself and your life. It's only by seeing it that you can come to know yourself as a whole person, rather than as a collection of labels and roles and body parts. Don't you want that for yourself – for every woman and girl?

How can we collectively do things differently? What lessons can we learn? What questions do we need to ask ourselves – and are we willing to be honest enough with ourselves in the answers? We can do this. One by one we can make a difference to ourselves and to our lives, and that will ripple out into the world around us.

The ripple effect

How can we make a difference to the huge issues of sexism, the patriarchy, misogyny or male violence against women just by changing the way we think about ourselves, by coming to think of ourselves first and foremost as human beings, then as powerful women? I know it might seem like a stretch of the imagination, but stay with me here.

Imagine you've started to see how you've been societally conditioned to behave, and look a certain way, to assess and judge yourself and other women against the standards of society. You've started to realise how much you see yourself through that lens. You begin to see the differences between who you are as a human being and all the roles and labels you've acquired throughout your life.

You've come to realise that you have far more worth than the way you look, and that you are just as deserving of love, respect and fair treatment as everyone else.

Don't you think you might start to feel differently about yourself? Don't you think you might start to feel better about yourself? Don't you think you might start to feel happier, or more confident, or experience more love and appreciation for yourself? Don't you think you might feel less driven by the demands of society, and feel more at ease in your own body? And if you start feeling like that, don't you think you might start to behave differently?

Now, if this happens, people are going to notice. You give off different vibes – subtly. You will be more comfortable in your own skin and own your space in the world, and others can't help but sense that, even if not consciously. And this all happens before you've even done anything directly to address sexism.

Some people in your life might not like sensing that you are a more powerful human being. They might feel threatened. But that's their problem, not yours. You're going through the most positive process you can for yourself, and that can only be a good thing. Others will be drawn to the difference they sense in you. That gives you the opportunity to tell them why you are different, about seeing things differently. Either way, keep on staying centred in your fundamental humanity, and feeling good about yourself.

The starting point

All that I've just outlined here is just a starting point. This step isn't an easy one, but it's the one that will make the most difference in your life. The more women who know their worth and come into their own personal power, the stronger and wider the foundation we can lay down, so we can build on top of it all the other things that will make a difference.

We have to start somewhere. As we've seen, how we've handled things to date has improved some things, but somehow others have become worse. So, let's look at where we are, and find out the next steps towards change. We can all play a part in that change.

CHAPTER 15

A way forward

What makes me think that I, you or any of us can make a difference in the way things are for girls and women?

What's the alternative? Are we content to do nothing? Are we just going to hope that eventually men will 'see the light' and things will change? Are we going to leave it all up to them?

Can we accept the status quo and do nothing when we can see what we've bought into, what we've tolerated, accepted and perpetuated? I know I can't.

In this book I present some ideas, some possibilities and some opportunities that will help us feel better about ourselves, feel that we have more agency in what happens to us, and that will give us better experiences of being a woman than we might have had previously. I want us all to have hope that things will be better for girls and women in the future, and confidence that we can each play some small part in that.

Reminders

The curse of the modern world is that we all lead busy lives. We're all juggling, and putting ourselves under pressure to do, do, do. I'm not about to ask you to add another load of things to your to-do list. As I mentioned earlier in the book, the most fundamental change you can make is wake up to how you have been conditioned and programmed.

These are some reminders for developing that awareness and understanding as you go about your day. It's about changing your perspective on your world – and on yourself. It's about seeing through a lens of awareness of what I've been talking about, and what you've come to understand. It's about being open to it as you go about your daily life and as you interact with others.

1. Start by noticing the sexism around you. Develop an antenna for it. You'll become more and more aware of it as you do. Also try to notice the sexism within you – and notice how you might condone sexism by tolerating or ignoring it.

2. Consider how your programming plays out in your life, and how you conform to society's expectations of you. Notice the straightjackets you wear in your life and think about which ones you might want to loosen.

3. Notice how you might be perpetuating the programming. Become more conscious of the words you use, and the examples you set.

4. Whether we are male or female, our cognitive dissonance has contributed hugely to where we are. Now that you see it, you can change it – for yourself and for future generations. Remind yourself that we can rewire our thinking and change our beliefs. Tell others about it.

5. Start to work on your attitude towards yourself. Notice your internal dialogue, which is actually the voice of your conditioning, that taught you to judge and criticise yourself and find your worth in the way you look. Remind yourself of this every time you look in a mirror. Build a sense of your own self-worth every day.

6. Get in touch with your own personal power. Grow it and become the magnificent woman you are. Claim your space in the world.

7. Start talking to others about all this – women, men, children. Speak up more, tolerate less. Have the conversations – even if they're difficult. As you do so, stand steady in your dignity and respect for yourself. This is what true equality is about – equality for all human beings.

8. As your sense of your personal power grows, begin to explore how you might want to – or feel compelled to – be even more proactive. Read more feminist books, look at websites, sign up for newsletters or join campaigns. Dare to believe that things can be different, and that you can be part of that difference.

9. Last, don't do all of these things once, or only for a few
   days, then forget about them. This is too important.
   Keep doing it. Repeat, repeat, and build on what you
   do. Remind yourself regularly of why you want to.
   Bookmark this page, or take a photograph of it, and
   come back to it again and again.

That's it. My best shot at a way for us all to make a
difference to our own lives, and for future generations.
Isn't it worth a shot? Of course, none of the above is going
to create any change overnight, or eradicate the ingrained
patriarchal conditioning in our culture.

If all it does is help to loosen its grip on you, if you
become more aware of your conditioning, if you judge
yourself less harshly and come to know yourself as a
powerful, valuable human being, then this book has been
worth writing.

Once you see how things are, you can't unsee it, but
that's just the start. At the very least, the process will help
you feel a lot better about yourself, and become more sure
about who you are, and comfortable in your own skin, but
you could gain so much more. You could give so much to
the girls and women who don't see it yet, and the boys and
men.

Remember all those occasions when we put up with
poor treatment just because we were women, all those
years we were treated as less than the intelligent, capable
people we are, just because we happen to be female. Know
that if you were the same person but happened to be male,
you would have had very different experiences. This is

sobering, and blood-boiling. This is the fuel we need to light the fire in ourselves – and the fuel I used to write this book.

I wrote it to try to make a difference to the experiences that my thirteen-year-old daughter will have as she goes through her teens and into her twenties, but it has turned out to have been cathartic for me – and galvanising. I'm talking about all this to you, and to anyone who will listen, and I'm going to keep talking about it and encourage others to do the same – women and men. I hope you'll do the same until we have all chipped away at the monolith that is the patriarchy, sexism, misogyny and male violence.

Are you with me?

ACKNOWLEDGEMENTS

First, a huge thank you to my brilliant editor Jane Hammett. I hope this is the first of many books that we work on together.

Also, many thanks to Mary Turner Thomson of The Book Whisperers for the typesetting and cover design, as well as her friendship and support. Also, a big thank you to Louise Welsh for reading early drafts, her invaluable feedback, and also proofreading assistance.

Finally, thank you to all my family and friends for being so supportive of all my writing endeavours: I really appreciate it.

And a special mention goes to my amazing daughter Annie. My love for you inspired me to write this book, to somehow try to make a difference for you in your future experiences of being a woman.

ABOUT THE AUTHOR

As well as writing and being an ambassador for Women's Enterprise Scotland, I'm also a partner in Supernature Oils, an artisan food production business, I volunteer with a homeless charity, and spend time with the people I love as much as possible. I write, I walk, I read, do yoga (badly), and meditate.

Connect with me:
www.lynnbmann.com
Twitter: @LynnBMann1 and @BEING_LBM
Facebook: Lynn B. Mann and BEING
Instagram: lynnb.mann and beinglbm

If you've enjoyed this book, I'd greatly appreciate you posting a review online please, either wherever you bought it, or on a readers site. It really does help other readers in deciding if it might be helpful/suitable for them. Thank you so much in advance if you do.

OTHER BOOKS BY LYNN B. MANN

BEING: Awake, aware, and experiencing life as your authentic self
(Being Books, 2021)
HBK ISBN: 978-1-8381628-2-5
PBK ISBN: 978-1-8381628-3-2

You know how to be a human thinking, and a human doing, but do you know how to be a human BEING?
Being isn't just the absence of doing. It's a dynamic place within you. Transform your experience of life by developing the ability to inhabit it. Discover how to cultivate the five states of Being and create all that your life can be – from your true self.
BEING is a practical roadmap and offers the antidote to the chaos that living in our head creates for us: psychologically, emotionally, physically, and spiritually.
In learning to inhabit Being, you will find:

- True rest and relaxation
- Mental peace and emotional equilibrium
- The true voice of your authentic self
- A sense of empowerment
- Your own vision and framework for how to create it
- How to fulfil the promise of your unique potential as a human being

BEING will inspire you to follow Lynn Mann's route, on your own transformative journey.
Whatever you want to achieve in life, you'll do it by first coming to live *in* and *from* BEING.

Being 21: Towards greater self-understanding in 21 questions
(Being Books, 2020)
HBK ISBN: 978-1-8381628-0-1
PBK ISBN: 978-1-8381628-1-8

'Who am I really?' What 21-year-old doesn't ask themself this question. Entering your twenties, turning 21, and the next few years, is an intense time in our lives. Supposedly it's when we become an adult. Where we begin to map out what our life might look like. When we're likely to have lots of big decisions to make around careers, studying, where we'll live, and in relationships. How are we meant to navigate all of this, if we don't really know who we are or what we want?

Being 21 is a beautiful book on the outside and meaningful within. This original and attractive 21st birthday gift introduces a process of self-questioning, which helps build confidence, and capability. It also supports mental and emotional wellbeing.

Throughout the process, the reader is helped in developing more: confidence, self-esteem, resilience, courage, adaptability, self-trust, and determination.

In 21 carefully crafted, powerful questions, former counsellor/therapist Lynn B. Mann has created a step-by-step guide towards the reader knowing more who they are, and what they want their life to be about.

NOTES

BEING A WOMAN

NOTES

BEING A WOMAN

NOTES

BEING A WOMAN

NOTES

BEING A WOMAN

NOTES

BEING A WOMAN

NOTES

BEING A WOMAN

Printed in Great Britain
by Amazon

31497627R00110